THE
DIVINE
feminist

THE
DIVINE
feminist

CERYN ROWNTREE

Paperback 978-1-913590-37-6
Ebook 978-1-913590-38-3

The Unbound Press
www.theunboundpress.com

Hey unbound one!

Welcome to this magical book brought to you by The Unbound Press.

At The Unbound Press we believe that when women write freely from the fullest expression of who they are, it can't help but activate a feeling of deep connection and transformation in others. When we come together, we become more and we're changing the world, one book at a time!

This book has been carefully crafted by both the author and publisher with the intention of inspiring you to move ever more deeply into who you truly are.

We hope that this book helps you to connect with your Unbound Self and that you feel called to pass it on to others who want to live a more fully expressed life.

With much love,
Nicola Humber

Founder of The Unbound Press
www.theunboundpress.com

*For Rachel and Josh Lavender, Kate and Sam Boldon,
and Josh and Ollie Curry. May we build a balanced
world in which you can all be wholly, beautifully
and powerfully yourselves.*

*And for my Auntie Irene, who bought the book
that made the dream come true.*

CONTENTS

INTRODUCTION

Our world is out of balance.

So far out of balance that we've almost forgotten there was ever an alternative.

An opportunity for as much rest as action,

To focus on fulfilment as much as success,

On art as much as science,

On community as much as competition,

And on power within, rather than power over.

It's time for things to change; for our world to come back to a place of sacred balance.

But that re-balancing has to begin with each and every one of us.

We know the age-old story of the oppression of the Goddess in favour of a patriarchal deity who would tell people exactly what they should and shouldn't be, in order to be considered "good" or "holy."

We know and have all experienced and witnessed the ways that same story has played out in the everyday, and continues to do so as those who identify as women – and many more besides – are oppressed, abused and put at risk by structures and institutions built to so clearly favour people who look a certain way, lead certain lives and were born into particular cultures and lifestyles.

But what if we were to take a step back from that story and look at the ways its biases and restrictions play out in each of us and in our world more broadly too?

Divine Feminism is about the energies that underpin this inequity; a way of seeing and being in the world that invites us to not only redress the ways those who identify as women are seen and treated within that world, but also to look deeper at the ways in which everything considered to be "feminine" has been positioned and treated as "less than" over the generations, lifetimes and centuries that have passed, and at the ways we and our planet are suffering as a result.

That's not to say that this is all bad news though. This book is an invitation to reconnect with those aspects within ourselves and the world; to tune back into each of them, and to reclaim the power and the beauty that they offer so we can begin to heal the wounds that centuries of imbalance have instilled upon us all.

The Divine Feminist is your invitation to turn inwards. To reconnect with yourself – with everything that you are, and find the place of flow and sacred balance that is truly right for you, leading you back not only to yourself, but also to a life that helps you remind the world there is another way.

It invites you to break down the dualities and the binaries our societies have inflicted upon us – concepts that can seem so desperately far apart and impossible to bridge at times – and instead consider what would happen if we, once again. combined those within ourselves and the world.

The end goal? To lead a charge that will change the world, combining the beauty and wisdom of the old ways with the knowledge and advancement of the new to create something that takes us forwards, together and in the wholeness of ourselves.

My story

I came to Divine Feminism at a time when I was broken.

Burned out from years of overworking and drained from a series of relationships that saw me giving far more than I was receiving.

Drinking to excess at least once a week so that I would feel confident enough to be out in the world, and bouncing from social engagement to social engagement because I couldn't bear to say no to anyone.

Then spending the times in between all of those things curled up on the sofa zoning out to movies and TV shows that convinced me life could be better than this, without ever giving me an understanding of how that could happen.

I had a wonderful family, good friends and a reasonably successful career but pored over self-help books in the hope of understanding the pulsing ache of not-enoughness that seemed to drive my every thought and action.

I'd always known there was more to life. Having seen and heard people no-one else could from a young age I was fortunate to be part of a family who recognised this as communicating with the spirit world and accepted rather than question or punish me for it. In my early 20s a series of spontaneous flashbacks to past lives explained more about my wounds and challenges than anything in my current life could make sense of and deepened my interest in that side of life, leading me to begin working consciously with all things spiritual. But spirituality was another escape; something I turned to when day-to-day life got challenging or when I felt too lost and overwhelmed to even recognise the next step on my path, never mind take it.

Things came to a head early in my 30s, when a drunkenly forgotten tampon led to a scare with toxic shock syndrome which made me decide it was time to work with, rather than against, my body and prompted me to buy a Mooncup, and a book on understanding my menstrual cycle.

I'd hoped to reduce cramps; maybe learn more about fertility along the way and definitely to see if I could somehow reduce the number of days a month when that cruel inner voice screamed, rather than whispered, its constant words of torment. What I found was a remembrance that went so much deeper than my menstrual cycle; deeper even than my own lifetime.

It took me back to one of the first past lives I had ever witnessed, as a priestess in Ancient Mesopotamia at a time when the world operated in line with those cycles and not against them. And it reignited memories of the destruction, abuse and peril I had seen as I witnessed the invasion of the place I'd called home, and the way that life had come to an end; memories that suddenly brought to the fore everything that had come since those times.

I saw generations before me tarred with a brush of not-enoughness simply because of who they were.

I felt the way that centuries of lifestyles built not on health and fulfilment, but on profit and productivity had taken a toll on the bodies of those generations and many that came after.

I recognised the way that our communities, and those around the world, had been torn apart by competition and a fight for supremacy under the idea that only the fittest survive.

I realised the clear patterns between that fear of survival and how it linked to the corruption in our societies, and the inequity that left so many groups of people struggling, suffering and dying in their droves, as others were able to sail through life far more easily simply because of the homes and bodies they'd been born into.

And I witnessed the impact all of those things had, not only on the human societies around me, but on the whole of our planet – from the animals suffering in captivity because we had come to see ourselves as superior to them, to the vital global ecosystems that were being cast aside and destroyed in favour of yet another money-making development.

These realisations joined the dots between every frustration I'd ever had with life on Earth; every inkling I'd ever had from spirit about the bigger themes that underpinned what I witnessed through them, and every cause that had ever left me weary and wishing I could do more. In many ways it made me want to curl up in a ball and hide...

But it also awakened a fire in me to change not only the way I lived, but also the way the whole world operated.

With that fire came a recognition of just how much I'd been bypassing myself and the life that was on offer to me; through meditation and focusing more on the spiritual world than I was the here and now; through the drinking that made everything in the real world seem more than a little hazy; and through the TV and movies that kept me distracted enough from the world around me to not feel the need to make any changes.

People talk a lot about the ways that a spiritual awakening impacted their lives, and my own experiences over the years can definitely back up that sentiment. Yet not one of those spiritual awakenings of mine have had anywhere near the impact of the experience that reconnecting back to my body had.

I sometimes think of the call to Divine Feminism as the product of my human awakening. The moment I realised that what I'd been searching for my whole life wasn't outside of myself as I'd always been led to believe, and that reconnecting with that something wasn't about rising higher, but about rooting deeper.

Deeper into myself and deeper into the Divinity that's available to all of us within this human experience, no matter how hard the world has tried to separate us from it.

Your journey

Maybe my story resonates with you, or maybe it doesn't. While we're all making our way through this experience of life here on Earth, not one of us experiences life the same way.

Maybe like I once was, you're drained, burned out and tired of feeling less than enough, as you desperately strive to tick off all of those boxes society tells you will be your one way ticket to happiness.

Maybe you've already ticked all those boxes, and are sitting in the shadows of a life you were always told would be enough, wondering why on Earth something feels so incredibly off-kilter and meh.

Maybe like me you've spent years of trying to bypass the physical self you've been told to disrespect and are now hearing the call inviting you to come home.

Or maybe you've grown tired of playing small; tired of listening to the voices of those who have abused and diminished you over the years and have felt a fire of your own ignite within you, reminding you that you are more than they'd have you think and driving you forward to show just what that means.

As a therapist who has not only taken this path of Divine Feminism for herself but has also supported countless clients through journeys to reclaim their own balance and wholeness, this book is my invitation to take your own steps further inwards on the road towards your own personal journey of reclamation.

Throughout the coming pages, I'll share the books and other media that have inspired me in that area of life, as well as exercises and meditations I've used with clients that are designed to help you reconnect with and rebalance these energies within yourself. It is my hope that some or all of them support you to deepen your experience of this book and all it encourages.

It also feels important to remind you that you don't need to read this book from start to finish. Each chapter is laid out in the order that feels right to me, but that's not to say they couldn't be read in all manner of different ways. If one section calls to you more than others then go there first; and if something doesn't feel right for today then by all means skip it and come back later.

My one request though is that you do come back to the chapters you miss at some point... All too often the things we avoid are those that might just hold the greatest gems for us, albeit hidden away inside of fears, shadows and discomforts we have done our best to avoid in the past.

A note on language

For a long time, what held me back from writing this book (and saw one full draft find a home in the depths of my computer's recycle bin!) was language.

The words "feminine" and "masculine" are such loaded terms that have been linked so closely to an idea of the gender binary that we almost can't see past them. For a long time I couldn't figure out how to write this book without using those words over and over again, despite the fact I was specifically not referring to biological sex or the constructs of gender.

What I am referring to is the energies that underpin those words; energies that could just as easily be referred to as yin and yang or Shakti and Shiva – both terms that I've avoided as they don't come from my culture; as dark and light – also now incredibly loaded words which miss a lot in terms of their energetics; or as receptive and projective – incredibly clinical sounding words that take me back to middle school biology classes! In many ways it feels as though the imbalance at the heart of this book has permeated the Western world so much that we barely have words – at least not in English – to even capture what we truly need to return to.

But as a practicing witch, there is one duality I talk about a lot, and its one that I feel fits the energetics this book is based upon well: the cyclical, connected energy of the Moon and the always-on, eternal light energy of the Sun. So, although we will discuss the "feminine" and "masculine" energies specifically within the first chapter, I will refer to lunar and solar energies in the pages that follow. It is my belief that we all possess each of these energies – and more besides – within us, and that our outward expression of those energies has no bearing upon who we are or how anyone else gets to define us within this world of ours. There is only one person in this world who should have the power to define us, or indeed to label the energies within us.

With that in mind, please know that when I speak of "women" or "men," I refer to the individuals who identify by those labels. I write this at a time when the ways in which our societies talk about gender is evolving and recognise that, as someone who lives life through a privileged lens of cisgender, there may be things I get wrong in the coming pages but want to be clear that I believe the imbalances I write about here are all part of the divisive and supremacist path that incredible LGBTQIA+ activists around the world are now trying to unpack, and intend this book to support rather than challenge that work.

As the name Divine Feminist may suggest, this book will also contain references to religion and spiritual traditions. I come to this work as a practicing witch, raised in a predominantly Christian society and will inevitably fall back on these traditions for my own work. That is not to say that good – or even better – examples cannot be found in other traditions or cultures, but only that I don't want to stake a claim to or misrepresent something that is not mine to define.

I write this book as an able-bodied white woman from the West – the North East of England to be specific. And although, like so many of us, I have suffered at the hands of the patriarchy, I recognise that my life in many ways includes a great deal of privilege. With that in mind, I don't claim to have all of the answers – or even all of the questions – but encourage you to continue your journey with Divine Feminism by learning more from and about writers, teachers and practitioners from not only mine or your communities, but also others across the world.

My hope is that the ideas contained here can be a starting point, for you and for many others besides, of an idea that can take hold and grow in a way which befits all of us and supports every person to grow, thrive and heal as exactly who they are, finding balance, fulfilment and support along the way and enabling our whole world to change for the better.

Additional materials

At the end of each chapter of this book you will find a list of journal prompts and exercises aimed at helping deepen your journey with this topic. You will also see the titles of at least one meditation and ritual for each chapter.

For the sake of space (no-one needs War and Peace!) I have chosen not to incorporate the meditations or ritual suggestions themselves within the pages of this book. However all of those, together with a number of other supporting materials, can be found on the Divine Feminist website at **www.divinefeminist.com/book-resources**

Please know that the meditations included in this book don't need to be done in silence on a meditation mat. If you find it easier to listen while walking, cleaning, gardening or doing something else entirely then please do so – just ensure you keep yourself safe throughout.

Creating a sacred space

This book is divided into five sections, each beginning with an invocation of the elemental energy most closely aligned with the coming chapters.

These sections exist to help create a sacred space within which the work of Divine Feminism can take place.

The elements are the building blocks of the natural world and working with them more closely can help us to build a deeper connection with the Earth and with our most primal selves. Upon reading each section's invocation, I invite you to sit with the elemental energy that rises up and consider how this feels within and around you as well as the images that come up to you.

Take the time to connect with each element as and when feels right to you as we work together to create that sacred space for wisdom and transformation.

HOW ARE YOU, HOW ARE YOU REALLY?

It's the way I start every episode of the Feminist podcast, and a question I invite you to turn to every time you pick up this book and every time you put it down.

There are subjects, stories and words within these pages that may spark emotions for you and others that may bring up some – and there's no simpler way to put this – serious shit. The imbalances I write about here have been used as weapons against us for generations, and reading about them in black and white may just trigger the wounds forged by those weapons within your current life, the lives of your ancestors and the wider experiences of your soul.

I make no apology for that because sometimes we need to feel in order to recognise what needs to be worked with, delved into and healed.

But that doesn't mean it's easy. Which is why tending to yourself as you work through and process all of this is important. I recommend reading with a snuggly blanket and a cup of your favourite tea; taking regular breaks to do the things that nourish your body and soul; breathing deeply as you move between pages and chapters and, of course, checking in with yourself with this all important question whenever you need to as you read.

In fact, this is an important question outside of the process of reading this book too, and if I had my way, this is a question we would ask ourselves regularly.

I live in the UK, where everyone is always about manners and social etiquette. Often when we see someone we know, the greeting will be: "Hello, how are you?" Before the two people then wander along on their way, without either ever really waiting for the answer.

It's a running joke in our society that people don't even *want* to hear the answer. Which is why so many reply "fine thanks," even if that's the last thing they're feeling.

But for so many of us, that's not just the glib answer we give outwardly. Often we're so busy tending to the needs of others, going about our day-to-day lives, and generally trying to keep ourselves going no matter what life throws our way, that we forget to even listen to the real answer for ourselves.

So right now, I invite you to read those words and let them flow into you – mind, body, heart and soul.

Listen for the response – feel for the response – in every part of yourself, and see what comes up.

And then ask a second question: And what do you need? Then see how you can respond.

If that response isn't something you feel you can give alone then always, always remember to seek support for anything that feels particularly tough or stingy. Where support feels particularly hard to come by, then check out the back of the book for details of the Divine Feminist community; a group of souls dedicated to exploring this path for themselves and supporting one another along the way.

BALANCE

SOLAR   LUNAR

In a book called The Divine Feminist, it seems only right that we start by talking about the first casualty of patriarchy; the Divine Feminine.

That story has been covered many times by many different people – including by some of my favourites included at the back of this book, so isn't something I want to repeat in full. But for those who haven't read it elsewhere, let me give you an overview of the tale I'm referring to.

Those books will tell you that once upon a time, the world worshipped a Goddess – the Goddess, in fact, the Great Mother – who was revered above all else. In many ways that's no surprise, the Goddess was aligned with those people who grow and birth life and whose natural cycles personified everything our ancient ancestors lived by. What could be more powerful or sacred?

Then patriarchy arrived; a force that decided the natural order of things wasn't quite as it should be and that a few changes here and there would create opportunity for much greater power and expansion.

But why would anyone listen to them when those changes meant going against, not only the natural order of the world, but also the goddess they held most sacred?

So they began spreading new stories, of a God or gods more powerful than the Goddess who exemplified the action-driven, focussed, dominant energy which was always striving to grow and win.

The spread of those stories and the belief systems they represented didn't happen in isolation; unsurprisingly they coincided with the empire-building and colonisation that modelled those same behaviours and, slowly but surely, began to take over the world.

Given where we find ourselves today I don't need to go into the damage that way of life caused – the abuse and disrespect of the Earth and its people, the displacement of so many from the lands they called home and held sacred, the dismissal of individual cultures and belief systems. So much of the world was and continues to be colonised by a force that physically disconnects us from nature, our ancestors and everything except those intellectual and physical powers it believed would allow humans to gain more and more power and control.

We know that story of power and control wasn't strictly true; that the forces behind those changes have been acting in the interests of an increasingly smaller group of humans who considered themselves worthy of those things – specifically white, able-bodied, sane, heteronormative, cisgender, well-educated, well-spoken, upper class, financially secure men. Meanwhile the rest of us have been segregated off, labelled and placed into boxes that entitled those in power to decide how worthy or otherwise we were and leaving many of us as desecrated, abused and forgotten as the Goddess herself.

It's a pretty simple story on paper; one with a good old villain to boo and hiss and a heroine in the form of the Goddess who we can all cheer on to victory and her rightful place of global domination, right?

Except that that's something I disagree with. And one I think our ancestors would disagree with too. Because as I see it, nothing begins with the Goddess alone.

A time of sacred balance

For as long as there has been a planet Earth, there has been the constant outward facing light of the Sun ruling the daytime and the ever-changing, inward facing energy of the Moon presiding over night. So from the very beginnings of our species, these two forces and their energies were revered.

So revered, that our ancestors in all cultures personified them into deities who guarded and presided over our world; with the cyclical energy of the Moon leading lunar deities to be cast as Goddesses while the always-on energy of the Sun led solar deities to be seen as Gods.

With that in mind, can you truly imagine a time when humans with nature-based belief systems worshipped the Moon and not also the Sun? The Earth, but not also the skies? To me that seems just as imbalanced as the opposite perspective, the place we find ourselves now.

Feminists are often accused of being "man-hating." And although there are plenty of men who have scared, hurt and upset me over the years, I know too many good ones to ever hate men in general or want them to be forced into submission in the way others in the privilege system have been previously. And while I would be intrigued to see a society based wholly in favour of the matriarchy, I don't see how that would be any closer to the sacred balance I so clearly see and feel us having once called home.

So although I can't speak for anyone else out there, when I advocate for the return of the Divine Feminine, it's not with the intention of those lunar energies overruling the solar completely, it's with the aim of siting them firmly beside one another and recognising both as important – for our Earth and for ourselves.

To do that means recognising that equity and natural balance within and around ourselves too; breaking down the dualities that have been used to decide our worthiness and coming back to a place of reconnection – with ourselves and everything each of us truly is. And with the glorious, flowing ecosystem of this planet we get to call home.

The feminine's lunar roots

I align lunar energy with what we know to be feminine, but unsurprisingly the truth of that energy is also a long way from what that word has come to mean, and from the feminine gender construct so many of us have grown up with. This energy is big, it is powerful and for those who come up against it, lunar energy can be downright scary. Which maybe explains a lot about why patriarchy tried so damned hard to diminish and control it.

But as with so many of the boxes that patriarchy has built for us, these definitions miss out on so much of what this energy truly is.

Consider for starters the way we've been told that "feminine" and "power" do not and cannot go together unless we are talking about Beyoncé.

Yet true feminine energy is powerful as hell; it is the energy of the dark and of the Earth; not only capable of conceiving, gestating and tending even the most delicate of new life with true care and tenderness, but also defending those lives with sheer ferocity.

This lunar-focussed energy is as seductive as the rhythm of waves against the shore and the light of the Full Moon as it shines upon us. Maybe this, more than anything, is what was once considered to be so terrifying to those in pursuit of power; the fact that in contrast to the physicality and rationality of the Sun, the power of the Moon lies in the emotions that welcome us in and have a tendency to bring us over to their way of thinking.

It is the energy of water; flowing with the natural rhythms that gives time for that deep inner work, as well as for stepping out to stand up for what they believe in. It recognises the connection of those cycles – a connection with humanity and with all of nature that brings joy and soul-bursting love, while also linking into the grief and pain that can be felt through those connections; emotions that, at times become too raw and too heavy to hold and erupt from us with the force of wildness.

I'm a self-proclaimed geek, and vividly remember unashamedly sobbing in the cinema when I watched both 2018's Wonder Woman and 2019's Captain Marvel movies. Why? Because I was so moved by their depiction of a power that was different to what society had taught me.

I was moved when Gal Gadot's Diana leapt high into the air and landed on the ground with a wobble of her thigh; with the recognition that there could be softness in strength.

And I was moved when Brie Larson's Carol Danvers realised that the way to tap into her full power wasn't through bypassing her human emotion but by embracing it, and allowing it to fuel her into action.

The lunar energy can be found in so many of the deities and archetypes that are worshipped and recognised throughout the world. But more than that, this energy can be found within each of us and the world that we belong to. Our challenge – and the invitation of this book – is to find a way back to that power and all it represents in a world that has worked so hard to diminish and other it.

Shining a light on the solar masculine

It often strikes me that a force so determined to diminish a force it considered competition probably wasn't as confident – or even strong – as it claims to be. The truth is that the originators of patriarchy were no stronger or braver than the playground bullies who are often some of the most scared people of all.

Patriarchy is not masculinity.

For all it might claim to revere those energies and behaviours it deems "masculine" and tip the scales in favour of certain groups of men, it has imposed just as many limitations on the true solar energy of the masculine as it has on the lunar and the feminine.

This isn't me apologising for misogyny, male violence or any of the shitty things men on this planet have committed in the past or still commit today. I've experienced those things for myself and supported countless friends and clients through them too. If I could click my fingers and erase one thing from the face of this planet, toxic masculinity would be right up there near the top of my list.

But toxic masculinity is not the truth of that energy we call masculine. Instead it is something that has limited and diminished so much of that energy, and forced those who identify as men into tiny, limited boxes which require them to hide so much of themselves away from the outside world. Away from themselves.

True solar energy is beautiful, powerful and so important to our world, if only we can dig past the conditions that patriarchy has imposed upon us.

It is the spark that drives us into action and the fuel that keeps us moving. It is the strength of the warrior and the dependability of the father; the clarity and intellect of the Air that allows us to plan and enables things to grow.

Solar energy has the assurance of a king, trusting itself and its counsellors to make wise decisions, and the wisdom of the sage to pursue only that which is true and focussed on a greater good.

There is an aggression and a sexuality in the Divine Masculine for sure, but those things are built upon a confidence that knows when to negotiate rather than fight and on a respect that sees sexuality as a shared energy rather than a dominant force.

In traditions across the world we see deities and archetypes who represent these traits in beautiful ways which honour the truth of the solar energy; a truth we need to return to within our communities and each of us, if we are ever going to save our world from the clutches of patriarchy.

That's hard to do. It's hard to even consider, when so much of the alleged masculinity we see today is violent, oppressive and terrifying; when so many of those who have abused and terrorised us in the past have done so under the banner of what they claimed was masculinity; and when so many of those who claim to be against that behaviour will state their case with cries of "not all men."

No, not all men. But enough.

Why? Because the systems and structures they grow up in are toxically imbalanced and have moved away from so many of the positive attributes that were once revered and celebrated, and have convinced us that masculinity means only one thing: a drive for dominance at all costs and a severing of anything that may be considered less than that.

A return to sacred balance

Perhaps one of the earliest crimes of the patriarchy was the ways in which it disconnected us from these energies, putting them into rigid little boxes that aligned specifically with biological bodies and the genders with which we were encouraged – and at times forced – to identify.

Patriarchy will often put it like this: Masculine energy was for those who identify as men, something that in many cases was allowable only for those who were biologically male; and feminine energy was for those who identify as female, with anyone who dares think outside of those boxes or embrace an energy society deems not to be "theirs" being persecuted.

We know that gender is nothing but a performance, and that the idea that our physiology is what makes us male or female is both ridiculous and undoubtedly just another way of restricting us from the wholeness of who we could be and truly are. But it is that division and restriction that is problematic, not the energies themselves.

Whatever names we give these energies the truth is that all of us – and indeed the whole world – embody both, and a whole spectrum in between and beyond the two, with the place of balance on that spectrum continually flowing at any given time.

But given how much power a union of those energies can hold, is it any surprise that we have been discouraged from recognising them within us. After all, if we take it back to basics, it is the union of the masculine and feminine energies and the qualities they represent that create human life.

I don't say that in a heteronormative way – again this is about energy, not people – because the truth that patriarchal belief systems have tried so hard to hide from us over the centuries is that every identity is not only valid and undeserving of shame or judgement, but that every identity is sacred. That all is sacred, throughout this energetic spectrum and beyond.

The union of the all is a theme you see reflected in a number of mystical traditions, not least nature-based belief systems such as my own.

You should know right away that witchcraft is one of the foundations from which Divine Feminism came, in no small part because of its approach to balance and equity. To the witch, everything is sacred, and power and Divinity run through everything, everyone and every place. Part of the beauty of being a witch is in recognising, connecting to and honouring all of that – not only every individual piece of the Universe (including ourselves) but also the overarching union of all that it represents.

Imagine a world where that was the norm. Where we all – regardless of our spiritual or religious beliefs – held everyone and everything in equal places of honour. Where we celebrated the differences between things, people and creatures and the beautiful individualities that each of those comprised. And where, all the while, we cherished and respected the glorious wholeness created when those individual facets come together, and the newness that is born as a result.

Another important aspect of witchcraft is balance. After all, what is ritual? A calling in of the elements to support whatever we are trying to attract to or diminish in our lives. Then a series of dedicated actions taken with the intention of rebalancing energies in and around us in order to make that happen. I know, when I put it like that, witchcraft sounds a bit less mystical and a bit more like some etheric science project, but it's a mindset that has really helped me in planning and carrying out more potent rituals over the years.

In many ways, this brings us back to the Divinity which makes this book different from your standard take on feminism; to the spark of creation and newness that many consider to be the Divine.

It's easy to think that the soulful side of Divine Feminism is a nice to have. Particularly when the inequality in our world right now leaves so many in a state of true danger, persecution and hardship. But for me, it is the lack of sacredness, honour and reverence for the truth of these energies which has allowed this world of ours to sway so badly out of balance and so far from the point of union.

I have vivid memories of lifetimes when those energies were seen as much more free-flowing; when the feminine and masculine were considered to be equally sacred and each of us were not only "allowed" to embody both, but were downright encouraged and revered for it. To think of those lifetimes never fails to nourish my soul and give my heart hope that we can get back to a place like that for ourselves.

Of course, it will never be the same as it was back in those ancient times. We and our world have moved on, so I can't tell you exactly how a future built on union and sacred balance will look or feel, but I can give you some pointers to find it, one of which comes from recognising the beauty and the sacredness that lives in a place of connection.

The First Key: SYNERGY

The key here is in finding the synergy; in recognising that so many of the binaries and dualities we have been sold are bullshit concepts designed to separate and restrict us. And in stepping back from this to see another way.

Synergy means to take two parts and look not just at their differences, or even at only the benefits that can be found when we combine the two, but at what can be created if we put the two together and allow them to stew in some glorious alchemical cauldron of wholeness, until we find the C that is created when A is added to B.

That synergy is how we step out of the boxes that patriarchy has placed us in. And start to bridge the divides that have led us into places of separation and oppression, within ourselves and within the world too – where it is long past time for us to celebrate the beauty in our diversity and the everything that we can create alongside one another.

Wondering where to even start looking for synergy? Consider the

Consider something as simple as a bee flying from flower to flower to collect nectar as food – a pretty basic, even selfish act you could say... Until you realise that the very act of flying between flowers transfers pollen, helping those plants to reproduce and keeping the plant species going just as it does the bees.

Bringing this even closer to home consider the alchemical synergy involved in baking a cake; putting together an egg, flour, milk, butter and sugar – all valid ingredients in their own right, but not necessarily all things you would want to eat solo, even if placed on a plate together. Combine them in a bowl and pop them in the oven though (or not, I can't be the only one who loves cake batter?) and you have something so much better than the sum of its parts.

It is time to remember that we are both the bee and the flower – able to meet the needs of the world around us while also having our needs met without either of us having to suffer; and that we – all of us – are the cake, so much greater than the sum of our parts.

EXERCISES AND PROMPTS

MEDITATION

Connect with the Divine Masculine and Divine Feminine within: This simple meditation will support you in becoming more present within your mind, body, heart and soul, and can be used whenever you need to come into the moment.

RITUAL

Lunar and solar connection: This ritual will help you connect with both the lunar and solar energies in preparation for moving through the rest of this book.

EXERCISES

- As you move through your day, pay attention to examples of synergy within your life and the world around you; the places where two or more parts create something so much greater than each of them individually.

- Take a few minutes each to sit outdoors under the light of both the Sun and the Moon (ideally when it is full). Close your eyes and soak in their energies, feeling as they fall upon your skin. How does that feel? What comes up in your body as these energies soak in?

JOURNAL PROMPTS

- What does balance mean to you?

- What does synergy mean to you?

- What are the dualities you believe to be true? If you were to consider each as a spectrum where would you find them?

- What do the ideas of feminine and masculine energy mean to you? How would it be if you used other words like solar and lunar, the Taoist yin and yang or the more practical receptive and projective? Would that change the meaning for you?

- How does it feel to consider yourself in relation to the energy elsewhere on that broad spectrum from your own gender identity? How about considering the energy that you identify most closely with?

- If you identify as gender neutral or non-binary then consider how each of those energies feel to and for you.

Please note that if this last prompt is particularly triggering to you then it is one to be avoided or worked through with support. We must keep ourselves safe and supported at all times.

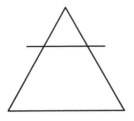

air

The breath of life, the winds of change and the whisper of inspiration.

Air is the thought that flows through us and shifts our perspective, moving us forward into a direction that could change us.

It is the gentle breeze on our face that cools and soothes when the heat of the Sun becomes too much to bear, and the stirring that shows what may have otherwise remained hidden.

We welcome Air from the East with the first light of the morning Sun; with the new life of Spring and the energy of the Maiden.

Spring is the mind, clear and pure, and full of wisdom.

With Air comes the inhale of the new, of freshness and of potential.

And with Air comes the exhale of release and the readiness to move forwards.

To ignore Air is to remain still, motionless, lifeless. It is to continue evermore in a state of restriction.

To restrict Air is to choose never to be refreshed, rejuvenated,

But to allow Air to roam free with no balance is to be in a state of perpetual movement; never able to lay down roots or take action.

It is to stay in our minds, stuck in the pressures of thought and unable to listen to the callings of our hearts or the wisdom of our bodies.

Air is wisdom and insight and deserves to live in balance.

And so we call to the East, and to Air. To the new of the Maiden, the Spring and the Moon.

We call to the birds and the clouds, to the bees and the winds, to the sylphs that dance on the breeze.

And we ask them to join with, to work with us and to bless us with their freshness, their inspiration and their clarity as we begin this journey to a state of rebalance.

To Air and the East, hail and welcome.

May it be so.

To hear this invocation in full along with a short story,
The Winds of Change, *visit the additional materials*
link at the back of the book.

EXPANSION

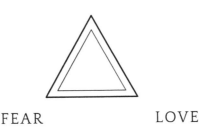

FEAR   LOVE

Back when I started moving in spiritual circles there was a saying which has become a bit of a cliché since: "There are two voices within you, love and fear, which will you listen to?"

The idea was that the voice of love came from your soul, it was eternally positive and would always have your best interests at heart. Meanwhile the voice of your fear? That was one to avoid, the voice that came from your ego and was doing its best to keep you small.

It wasn't a bad theory – after all there are always multiple paths we can follow in a world that has done so damned much to keep us small; there are paths that offer expansion and growth and those that are rooted in contraction and stuckness.

The problem was that by naming those paths love and fear, or for that matter by aligning them with our soul and our ego, we are massively oversimplifying their roles in that way our logical, limited minds have a tendency to do and, in doing so, are paving whichever road we take with uncertainty.

In the years since I first heard that theory, the idea of love vs fear, or soul vs ego has morphed in so many ways, each more limiting than the last and each offering one more reason for so many of us to criticise and second-guess ourselves.

"Whatever someone does to you, send them love and light. Remember they are always a reflection of you."

OK, but does that mean we can't call out bad behaviour, or recognise and walk away from those people and situations that really aren't for us?

"Positive thinking is the only way to bring good into your life – think or speak anything other than what you want to attract and it will never come your way."

OK, but what happens to the thoughts that are less than positive if we don't acknowledge them? Do they just sit within us and fester instead? And does that mean that someone with, say, OCD who is plagued by intrusive thoughts can never attract good into their lives?

"The voice that doesn't come direct from your soul is only ever trying to keep you small and should be ignored."

Sure, but when it tells me not to waste my time on clothes, when making my way into town is priority for the day then you know I'll get arrested, right?

There is so much merit in positivity. As an optimist that is something I believe with every fibre of my being. But positivity cannot be our every thought and action. Not only is that unrealistic, but it diminishes so much of our power.

And there is a definite danger in allowing ourselves to be ruled by a voice or belief system that keeps us small – hell, it's that very certainty which drove me to write this book! But that's not to say that we should never listen to a voice of caution when it stirs within us.

Facing our fears

Fear can keep us small, there are no two ways about that.

This book took me years to write, largely because I was terrified of sharing my voice. Scared that what I wrote wouldn't be good enough, or that I would say the wrong thing, cause offence to someone I was trying to support or engage with, or miss some critical point which meant that lifetimes of work to understand and overthrow the patriarchy would be wasted and I'd have to start from scratch again.

I know, the voice of my own fear is both very loud and super intense!

The reality, of course, is that some of those things could happen; you could be reading this book right now hideously annoyed or offended by something in these pages, or could put it down a few chapters from now entirely unmoved and tell friends, "Nah, no need to bother with that one, it's rubbish." Maybe I'll read back the finished version of this book and think, "Dammit, I completely forgot to mention…" (at which point, watch this space to learn more about the Divine Feminist 2.0, headed your way soon!). Maybe I even need to accept that this book will not be the single key to unlock what a wise woman once told me is my soul's mission.

But are any of those things a good enough reason not to go ahead and write the damned book? Hell no. As Taylor Swift said in a speech

I watched while editing this chapter: "If you're being met with resistance that probably means that you're doing something new. If you're experiencing turbulence or pressure, that probably means that you're rising." So in those cases what do we do? Let that resistance, turbulence and pressure hold us back? Or just keep on rising and wait for our ears to pop back again?

I choose the latter. And I'd wager that if we want to break down centuries-old patterns of oppression and free ourselves and the world from the cages of patriarchy and so many of the wounds that force has inflicted upon us in this life and others, we all need do the same.

But that's not to say fear is always something that is trying to keep us small. If we consider it through Freud's lens of the ego – something many in the spiritual communities like to do – then it is often the inner voice that is trying to keep us safe, offering up opportunities for discernment when it fears we will otherwise throw ourselves into something dangerous.

And while some of those things may well be dangerous because they are challenging old wounds that have held you back, others will just be downright bad ideas.

To dismiss the voice that questions or opposes anything that sounds positive is to take away the opportunity for us to really consider the repercussions of our actions and the wider context of our choices at any given time.

But more than that, to reduce the voice of "fear" to something that is trying to keep us small, removes so much of the nuance of soul work, suggesting that the choices our soul is calling us towards will always be smooth, with no pain or challenge along the way.

In her book *Daring Greatly*, Brené Brown writes of how some of her most vulnerable experiences have been kissing her sleeping children goodnight and being hit with an unspeakable wave of love that was immediately followed by a wave of terror that something may happen to them. Here in the West, we aren't so good at the love without attachment that many Buddhist teachers speak of, meaning that love and fear can so often go hand in hand just as Brené suggests. Does that mean we should avoid having children because the idea of such great love is terrifying? Of course not.

Equally, in a world that has done so much to persecute anyone who steps out of the box of "normality," of course our fears can go hand in hand with the big, expansive truths our souls want us to follow. But imagine if we avoided everything that triggered that fear of persecution? We would miss out on so much opportunity.

Just like anything that waits in the darkness, our fears are much scarier and have much greater power when we refuse to look straight at them. But when we stop to get to know those fears of ours we start to recognise so many of them for what they are; protectors for these mortal bodies, fallible minds and delicate hearts of ours. And when we don't pay attention to those protectors, they will only fight harder and find different tactics to be heard.

Is that to say we should listen to our fears ahead of everything else? Gods no. But for all too long we have been told to wage war against our fears as some sort of evil, invading force. My suggestion is that we work with them instead, negotiate until we can discern their truth from the noise they are making too.

One of my favourite decks of oracle cards, Colette Baron-Reid's *Wisdom of Avalon* oracle includes a card called fear, within which is something that has always stuck with me – an invitation to write a list of your fears with the reminder that when we do that, we will often find "that what we are afraid of is fear itself."

Is love the way?

I am *all* for spreading the love. I dream of a world where people care about one another as much as they do themselves, and empathy is one of the fundamental principles of what I consider to be my life's work.

But. There has to be a but.

There are people who hurt us, abuse us and cause us great trauma. To suggest that we "send them love" and all will be forgiven, is bypassing our healing to the max.

What's more, to tell a victim of trauma to send love and light to someone whose actions have fundamentally shifted their life in painful ways? Disrespectful and dangerous.

And honestly, anytime we send a love that is laced with bitterness and fury into someone else's energy, that won't exactly be a gift to them; nor to us as we try to regurgitate our original feelings for that person wrapped up in a gritty, sparkly glitter that will scratch our hearts and our throats on the way out.

As someone who tries to abide by the law of, "Treat others as they want to be treated," a practicing therapist and a witch who holds the Wiccan Rede – the closest thing we witches have to a rule book – close to her heart, I am not suggesting that we should go about the world sending out hatred or bad vibes to anyone who hurts or pisses us off. After all, the Wiccan Rede does remind us that what we put out into the world will be returned to us times three, while ending on the powerful line: "Eight words the Wiccan Rede fulfil: And ye harm none, do what ye will." Or, in other words: "It all comes down to this: Do whatever you like, as long as you don't hurt anyone."

However, I do firmly believe there is a middle ground between that and sending love; that it is absolutely OK to remove ourselves from a person or situation and choose not to engage with someone whose energies are not a good fit for ours. And that it is downright acceptable to speak and stand up against bad behaviour when we witness it.

That's not to say people should be written off without an opportunity to change, grow and make amends. But it is important we recognise that some things cannot and should not be tolerated, and that to choose to speak out or to walk away and release a situation rather than forgive it with love does not make us somehow "bad" or "less than," but often means we are caring for ourselves and those who are important to us.

Love is a wonderful thing that this world could certainly do more of, but to focus solely on love can be incredibly restrictive and damaging, even when that force is coming from within us.

To listen for a voice that is solely love-filled, after all, is to listen for something that will never make you feel in any way uncomfortable or scared. It is a voice that will wrap you up in a cosy blanket and tell you which way to turn for everything to be just fine. But that cosy blanket can dull out so many important sounds that we need to listen to, preventing us from healing the wounds that seem too painful to tackle and keeping us from the actions and decisions that might be initially challenging no matter how much benefit they have the potential to bring afterwards.

Sometimes the most love-filled things we can do involve stepping back from a situation or relationship that is no longer right for us – even as doing that causes the kind of pain and suffering we would give anything to do without.

And it's important to remember that the path of love isn't always one that is gentle or soft; sometimes the deep and fierce power of love will drive us to take actions we had never considered and to do things we didn't think possible. Like the people who find themselves lifting cars to save someone they love and the wild animals that are most ferocious of all when you get between them and their young, the path of love sometimes looks precisely the way you least expect.

Choosing the path of expansion

The true voice of our soul isn't one that speaks solely in the voice of either love or fear, but it does always have our most expansive interests at heart. This is a voice that is loaded with wisdom and surpasses so much of what you consciously know. This in itself can be terrifying – that place of not-knowing, taking you straight into a path of both freewill and learning that has the potential to take you further than you would ever have imagined otherwise, if you'd stuck to a safe and obvious path.

Sometimes the path that is best for our souls isn't the one that seems to bring us love to start with, but instead involves that wise voice telling us to walk through what seems like fire and brimstone. This is where we must understand the nuance between those two voices, because otherwise it's all too easy to believe we're listening to the "wrong" one.

For the longest time, that fear of listening to anything but the positive voice kept me from making some seriously powerful choices... and at times from making any choice at all. I would go to make a decision, only to realise the dialogue that was going on inside me was much more complex than a simple love vs fear conversation.

Maybe the path I really wanted to follow made me feel squirrelly inside but sounded positive, while the one that brought most peace in my gut was exactly what I didn't want to do.

Or maybe the voice that represented the easy path forwards felt draining, while the opposite voice excited and energised me.

Then there were the times that both voices sounded fear-filled and left me with absolutely no clue which would involve me playing small and which would mean me doing my thing.

Those inner voices of ours aren't a binary of love and fear or black and white. Sometimes the voice trying to diminish us does so in a sweet and love-filled way that whispers all the things we want it to say, while the voice that speaks our truth weirdly agrees with the social conditioning we have, for so long, felt we should avoid.

To call this a debate between the good guys of love and the bad of fear, like some sort of devil and angel on your shoulder, is simplistic to the point of dangerous. But what if instead we thought about this as a spectrum of expansion and restriction? There are times the path of expansion will mean walking first through a tunnel that seems to squeeze us tight enough to take our breath away; and others when the cage of restriction will be gilded in a way that seems to promise freedom. But only we can decide which path to take or which cage to pause in while we catch our breath and decide our next steps.

There are no definitive rights or wrongs on this journey, only ever the choice to keep moving, growing and expanding in the best way we know how.

The Second Key: COURAGE

To pursue that path of expansion, we must practice courage; a word that is routed in the French terms of "strength of heart" and that my wise friend Sarah Beth tells me was once the name of the Strength card in tarot.

For those unfamiliar with the tarot, the card usually shows a woman standing side by side with a lion, her hand on their head. It encourages us to remember the power we have within us to stand side by side with the most ferocious of beasts, if only we can pause our own fears and animal instincts for long enough to connect with that true power first of all.

Courage asks us to get quiet and ask what the next expansive step is for us. And to follow that call, even when the rest of the world is shouting at us to do something else.

At times, that will mean pausing to tend to ourselves and go gently as we navigate the terrain of our inner wounds and their protectors.

And at others, it will mean looking those protectors in the eye, even as the words of caution they share with us sound genuine and love-filled, and giving them thanks. Then stepping forward with our jaws set and – as a good friend of mine would say – Just Fucking Doing it.

EXERCISES AND PROMPTS

MEDITATION

Meeting the guardians of your fear: Join me on a journey to safely connect with the guardians that are currently keeping us from working through and with our fears.

RITUAL

Welcoming in courage: Best done at the time of the New moon, this ritual will deepen your own strength of heart and support you in working with your own courage more fully.

EXERCISES

- Tune into that feeling of expansion within you; how does it feel in your body, mind, heart and soul when you are restricted and how about when you are in the opposite position? Consider some of the activities, places and people who help to put you into that place of expansion.

- What is something you could do today to choose a path of greater expansion? Maybe this is something small, like writing in red in rather than black pen, or wearing bright lipstick, simply because it makes you feel good.

JOURNAL PROMPTS

- Take some time to list your fears. Then ask why you are scared of these things. What is it you're truly afraid of underneath? Consider which of these are truly scary, which are based on past experiences, which are outside of your control and which you can take action to prevent. This is not about invalidating your fears, but about sorting through them to understand where we can get to know them better?

- Consider the idea of the danger in safety; what are the choices you could make or have made that feel safe on the surface but lead you down a path of restriction?

- What does courage look like to you? What are the most courageous things you have ever done?

- What are your greatest hopes and dreams? Take some time to journal on those and on the fears that keep you from pursuing them. How many of those fears could be approached or worked through from a different perspective?

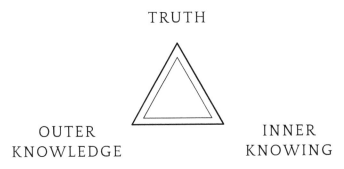

There are many things I am grateful for in this modern age, but as a geek who thrives on learning, search engines are right up there.

The answer to almost any question just a few taps or clicks away? People 200 years ago would have thought that was impossible, those 200 years earlier would have called it witchcraft and those a few centuries before would have scratched their heads and asked why we needed an "Internet" to answer questions.

I love the Internet and have so much to be grateful for in our online world. But I also wonder how far this age of outer information – of not only search engines but also books, TV shows, podcasts, radio shows, movies, seminars, conferences, newspapers, workshops and magazines, for starters – has taken us from our inner knowing.

In a world so full of outer noise, how do we get quiet enough to even tune into that inner knowledge? And at a time where there seems to be an expert – or many experts – out there on every subject, it is all too easy to think that we will never have answers that are worth listening to.

It took me five years to write this book, and almost as long to start the podcast of the same name. Not because the ideas weren't there or because I didn't believe the message of the Divine Feminist was one that could and would benefit the world but because, so much of that time, I felt I didn't know enough to talk about this. In a book that touches on politics, religion, history, science, business, spirituality, consciousness and social justice, I felt far from an expert on many of those things.

And this is one of the downsides of that overload of information we all have access to: it can stop us sharing our own knowing for fear of getting something "wrong" and prevent us from stepping outside of what anyone else has to share, to be able to recognise what we do know and trust, while also leaving us like deer in the headlights of all of the available information, with no idea of where to even start our journey of learning.

But is this any surprise, when we have spent so long being taught to look outside of ourselves for the "best" source of information, all while being disconnected from and told not to trust the easiest and closest information source of all?

I would say not. In fact, I would go so far as to say it is neither a surprise nor a coincidence that in a world ruled by those who are determined to suppress the more lunar-focused energies, we have gone so far down the path of outer information that we barely know how to connect with our inner knowing.

Information from outside

That's not to say that information from outer sources is all bad, or is some new-fangled thing enforced upon us by patriarchy and their technological whizz-kids. We have always shared information.

From my Nanna's recipe for ginger biscuits to the case studies of success and challenge from those who have gone before us, information has always been passed to us from our families, the people who have lived in the areas we call home, done the same jobs as us, studied the same subjects or practiced the same spiritual traditions. And while some of that insight is shared unconsciously as we mentioned before, some is definitely taught and communicated very consciously and found outside of ourselves.

There is and has always been a great web of universal knowledge available, the difference is simply in how we tap in, upload to and learn from that information.

Once upon a time that was done through word of mouth, Barbara Ehrenreich writes in *Witches, Midwives and Nurses* about the ways in which wise ones in each community would have taken trusted trainees under their wing and, bit by bit, passed on everything they knew. That still happens today; we undertake apprenticeships or are mentored by those willing to share their insights and expertise with us. Often when I work with mentoring clients those people they have learned from and been supported by are something I ask a lot about, because our role models and teachers can be some of the most important people in our lives.

But sharing information today is different, even when it comes to apprenticeships. Some of those differences are positive. The printed word made it possible for people to share their insights more widely, a reach extended even further by broadcast media and the Internet. And what a gift it is to be able to read and hear – sometimes directly from the teacher – the experiences of those who have gone before us no matter where and when we are.

However, that's not to say that the widespread sharing of information is all positive. Once upon a time, those wise ones would have chosen exactly who should have access to their teachings and insights, while now it can much more easily fall into the hands of those who aren't ready to receive those teachings, have the wrong intentions for it or simply are unsuited to work with it. There is no denying that a large part of cultural appropriation, for example, is down to information – some of it deeply sacred – falling into the hands of those who neither understand its context nor respect it.

As a white woman, there is a lot I will never be able to understand or talk to on that subject, but even I can tell you how frustrating it is to see people turn traditional festivals like the celebration of the thinning veils at Samhain into overly commercialised Halloween parties with no real respect for the traditions they are borrowing. That angers and upsets me and I am not someone whose ancestral land has been stolen from them or whose people are still abused today for their heritage, culture and practices, so I cannot begin to imagine the pain and disgust that comes from other communities coming up against widespread cultural appropriation.

Then there are the gatekeepers. We hear about how the printing press changed the world, but we must remember that was never the case for everyone, with formal education limited even today for many women and for those who are poor, Disabled, Black, Indigenous or members of other oppressed communities. As the sharing of written information became more widespread, so many were cut off from accessing that because of literacy, academic qualifications or financial factors. Even now racist, sexist and ableist institutions continue to deny or limit access to further education and particularly subjects covered within those fields. Meanwhile similar challenges are in no small part why so much wisdom from women and from BIPOC communities and other oppressed groups was lost to time, because many of those who knew the value of this information were unable to publish it, or even write it down. And this is without considering those things that the dominant groups in our societies considered inappropriate or illegal, such as the experiences of LGBTQIA+ people in so many parts of the world.

We are so often told that history is written by the victors, so why wouldn't the patriarchal, capitalist, ableist, heteronormative, white supremacist, monotheistic societies of the West share knowledge with us through exactly that lens?

Meanwhile Her stories and Their stories tend to be found elsewhere, passed on orally or shared as myth in sources we have been told are invalid. But I wonder how much wisdom and insight could be found if we were to treat those less formal sources with the same curiosity, respect and discernment?

Reconnecting with our inner knowing

In discouraging us from turning inwards for insight and information, the word has disconnected us from so much of our own instinct and wisdom.

Like the times we have successfully done something before or even have a hunch on how something should be done because of a natural affinity we have always had, but turn away from that insight and experience because we've been led to believe we're unqualified to give that insight.

Or the times we've sought information from every friend, family member, colleague and stranger on the Internet we can find, before making the decision we knew was right for us all along; or worse, before listening to their opinions in favour of the inner voice that is trying to shout at us.

But there are many answers that can be found away from Google if only we learn to cultivate the connection to ourselves to be able to hear that wisdom, and the confidence in ourselves to be able to trust it.

We hear so much today about our intuition, and as someone who has worked consciously with the spiritual and soulful realms for almost two decades now I know how much insight and support can be found if we tune into those subtle voices that arise from within us. In many ways, it was my early days of standing up in spiritualist churches to pass messages on from guides and ancestors that helped me to connect to my own inner knowledge; if these spirit people were sharing information through my inner sight, hearing and physical sensations that their family members later confirmed to be true, then surely it was possible that some consciously unknown force within me could and did share valid information through those senses too?

I'd like to tell you that led me to trust my inner knowing straight away; that I never doubt anything I hear internally and always back myself 100% but that is definitely not the case! Even today there are still things I find myself opening the web browser on my phone, or turning to one of the many unread books on my shelves to look for back up or confirmation rather than trusting what I already know to be true no matter what anyone else says.

Around about the time this book first began to take shape in my brain, I started to be told about something called Primal Healing.

I'd never heard the term before and no matter how many Google searches I did or healing books I read, was completely unable to find insight on what this term meant or how in the hell I went about doing it. For years that meant that it went on the back burner. Fast forward to 2021 and I began to piece together what this was all about; I saw things in meditation, made notes while journaling, and at every step would be led to conversations where one tiny fragment of that would be backed up in the most synchronistic of ways. Eventually I took the hint and asked a couple of friends if I could practice on them, with really exciting results; exciting enough that I will finally be offering Primal Healing to clients by the time you read this book.

I wonder how many new things are waiting within us to be birthed; held up by that societal conditioning that has told us someone else knows better, or that it's only ever a good idea if it can already be found in a book? I wonder how much more we could offer to the world and one another if only we had the confidence to turn inwards and share the best of what we found there?

This doesn't mean I believe all of that information to be solely ours to access or share either. Just as the Internet offers us a mass of external information that we can tap into for answers and insight at any given time, I firmly believe our inner knowing have access to wider sources of information than those of our own soul and intuition too.

Consider Carl Jung's focus on the huge source of unconscious knowledge that has been building throughout the whole of natural history in our collective unconscious leading to many of our dreams and beliefs; and the growing field of epigenetics which shows that the traumas we experience can be carried through our genes to physically and emotionally impact the people who come later, like the descendants of communities who suffer famine and find themselves suffering from the after-effects of malnourishment generations later.

Then there are the more spiritual sides of collective information, such as the Akashic Records, that contain all of the information we could ever imagine about everything that has ever happened and will ever happen to every soul in the Universe, and the grids of the Earth. They contain more information about the history of this Earth than our species has ever managed to uncover – or possibly will ever manage to uncover – through digging into the Earth itself. It might seem strange to list those things; information sources you can't exactly tap into through Google or your local library, but it feels important to remember that not all of the information sources we tap into outside of ourselves can be found tangibly. Just as with so much of the information our ancestors shared with one another, many are held in very different sources and passed on in ways that much of the modern world is either too busy to stop and consider, or has been told to discount, simply because it can't be academically referenced.

That's not to say we need never seek insight, guidance or education from external sources. Let me say for the record that I *strongly* discourage you from performing brain surgery or nuclear science without formal training from an expert! Our inner knowledge can lead us towards so many of the right answers, but it does not know everything, or at least not well enough to discount study, training and experience entirely.

There is always the possibility that our inward focus will have been swayed by the input of other sources over the years. How often has the voice that tells you not to do something sounded more like a parent or old teacher than anything you yourself would actually say? And even when the insight is wholly our own, we can still miss something crucial along the way, whether consciously or otherwise. From a conscious perspective, there are the motives we take into any conversation, ideas session or search for answers. Are you truly turning inwards with the intention of finding the right answer for you, or is there even a part of you stuck so firmly in a mindset of what you want that agenda to be that you will struggle to hear the alternative? We've all been there.

That's why stepping away from our inner knowing – either just to give ourselves some space or to run them by someone we genuinely trust – can be so beneficial for giving us just enough of perspective to be sure that we are speaking from a place of our own truth and, when it comes to using that information for the good of other people, that we are doing what we need to keep those people safe.

After many years of considering it and questioning my motives, last year I began a master's degree in Consciousness, Spirituality and Transpersonal Psychology (yes, it is just as complicated as it sounds! Imagine a little mind blown emoji right here). As much as I enjoy the learning and the opportunity to be a spiritual geek, possibly my favourite part of studying is the insights I'm gaining from reading the research, findings, theories and hypotheses of other people; and considering how those tie into and give a different perspective on the inner knowings I have long carried around on those subjects. These perspectives, in the long run, can only complement the things some part of me knew to be true long before I picked up a book on the subject.

None of us have all of the answers to this giant puzzle we call life – not even those who have placed themselves and their institutions at the very top of the power pyramid, no matter how much they would like us to think otherwise. But we do each have some of the answers to that big picture puzzle, and certainly more than just some when it comes to ourselves and our own lives.

Talking truth

None of this means that every piece of information we receive inwardly or from outside of ourselves can be wholly trusted of course. We know only too well that's not the case, and that many things considered to be "fact" in the past have long since been proven as incorrect or even dangerous.

But then they aren't the only ones; I write this at a time when there is a lot of talk about how science cannot be trusted. The agendas of those funding research of many types are at times questionable, leading to some... *interesting* outcomes. But we cannot forget that there are also good researchers out there whose agenda is to help people and advance our understanding of the world. Just as there are and have been many people over the years without access to labs and expensive support teams who still carried out excellent research and came to brilliant conclusions, and many others with dubious motives trying to call the shots when it came to deciding what should be deemed "true."

Then there are those on the other side of the fence too, some of whom speak out to challenge science from a genuine intention to help and support those around them. But some of whom take this stance from a completely different perspective; one rooted either in their own personal fears or in their drive of a different agenda they would like to be seen as "true."

That's an interesting word isn't it? We hear a lot about how ours is a "post-truth society," a term I have always hated since I feel it points a lot of fingers at things it suggests we shouldn't trust. And as you may have already gathered, I'm not someone who believes we should wholly dismiss anything simply because we can't trust everything.

But the more I think about it, the more I come back to the realisation that truth is very different to what we have always been told. Not because nothing is in any way true, but because everything we see has an element of subjectivity to it and requires consideration – requires us to turn inwards and ask who this is true for.

Each of us experiences the world differently by nature of our background, fears, hopes, dreams and so much more besides. As someone who has worked extensively with both communications and psychology, I've learned the hard way that although we can control how a message is sent, we can never control how it will be received; what will trigger a wound, make someone laugh, inspire an idea or fall on barren ground. Yes, there are things we can do to try and invoke certain reactions, and the more we know someone, the more we can understand them and get a better idea of what their response may be. But we can never know for sure.

Of course, we can say with some certainty that the sky looks blue and the grass green, but we can never be sure that someone else – even someone with full colour vision – will see the same shade of blue. And nor is that something we can measure.

Maybe post-truth isn't about saying that everything is fiction, but instead asking us to consider the nuanced idea of what is fact, and reminding us to consider the different agendas and experiences that lead us to a place of recognising truth.

Often that means filtering out what we categorically know to be rubbish within us and questioning those things that are subjective rather than objective – which, by the way, is almost everything!

Then it means acknowledging that what is true for us may not be something everyone else necessarily agrees with or experiences for themselves.

When all of that is done, we can ask ourselves what we know to be true. We can ask and wait for the answer long enough to understand what really does and doesn't feel true to us; listening to our minds, our bodies, our hearts and our souls to be sure. And then we sit with those answers.

That can be hard to do, particularly when your own process of deduction seems to have steered you wrong in the past. There are many past decisions I've gotten angry at myself for after getting them "wrong;" yet I realise now just how many of those decisions were made, not because they felt true to me, but because I let myself be overly swayed by other people's opinions or experiences, or by what society told me I should be doing.

That point of our own truth can at times be difficult to access, particularly with so many sources of information waiting to distract us from it. And even when we spot it, that truth can be difficult to stand in, with so many people ready and waiting to pull us away. But the power that comes from recognising, standing in and speaking from that place of your own truth is worth every dangerous step of the journey to get there.

The Third Key: DISCERNMENT

The key to finding our truth, and even to following it at any given moment, lies in cultivating discernment. Whether with academic papers or fireside tales, inner urgings or the things we believe to be true, the only way to find the point of our own truth is to step back and truly discern what each of those sources are telling us and why.

It can be tough to do that, particularly when we are lost or feeling in some way insecure. In many ways, that's why I trained as a therapist. While practicing as a medium, I saw so many people who were grieving or otherwise feeling lost and would accept any information they were given as true, simply because they wanted something to hold onto. That led to some pretty bad information being received as fact, and quite possibly followed through on by people who really needed a safe space to heal and reconnect with themselves before they looked anywhere – in or outside of those selves – for information from a place of grounding and discernment.

Discernment requires us to come back to ourselves first and foremost; to get intimate enough with that sense of truth within ourselves that sources of information. In a society that has tried so far to disconnect us from that sense of inner knowing and led us to believe that we are worthy of so little trust or faith in ourselves that can take time; time, support and a safe space in which to think.

But once we remember that place of truth, we can start to approach those many sources of information from a very different perspective. The key is not to dismiss any of them out of hand, but instead to give each of them the space to be heard, and then take the time to truly discern what each of those things mean to us, where they are coming from and what they're trying to say.

Those questions alone will allow us to dismiss some things right out of hand; a fast food company telling me that burgers and fries every day are a perfectly healthy meal? Hmm. And that guy on Bumble assuring you that you would be an excellent match even as every answer in his profile makes you cringe? That doesn't take a lot of discernment to figure out.

Others though will need a deeper dive; they will need you to tune into the feelings that these things bring up within you – not just emotionally but physically too because so often our body is closer to a place of our own knowing than our mind, and their responses are a brilliant tool to use when tapping into our powers of discernment.

Or you will need a conversation with someone – or maybe a couple of someones – you wholly trust to provide wise counsel. My mum is one of my favourite people to speak to whenever I'm stuck trying to discern the truth in a situation; not because she always agrees with me – there are a few things we have very different opinions on! But because she will ask the questions that I will often forget to ask –

questions that will always give me new perspectives through which to tune into that same sense of truth within myself.

I believe we can never practice discernment too much. Practice it whenever you read a book and connect with what feels true for you; whenever you listen to a news broadcast and unpick the facts from the agenda of that particular channel; and whenever you meet new people, asking whether your discomfort with them is because of past experience or societal conditioning, or whether this is a knowing that the person isn't a good fit for you.

It feels important to note here that discernment is different from judgment. Judgment is about decreeing what is right generally – about trying to make universal truths from the things that we or our societies have told us are right and wrong and criticising people accordingly with no consideration for their own personal truth, while discernment is about understanding what is right for us personally and taking action on that which comes not from owning our own truth enough to step away from what would restrict us, and towards that place of expansion.

EXERCISES AND PROMPTS

MEDITATION

Activating your inner cauldron of discernment: Together in this meditation, we will plug into and activate your Soul Centre – the centre of your soul in your physical body – and will activate the cauldron of wisdom and discernment that offers.

RITUAL

Calling back your inner knowing: This ritual prompt will support you to call back and tune into your own inner knowing and is best done around the New or First Quarter Moon.

EXERCISES

- This exercise, based on one from Richie Bostock's book *Exhale* is a simple way to connect with the voice of your truth. Very simply say – out loud or in your head – something you know to be true. Repeat it to yourself and then take a couple of deep breaths in and out as you notice how that breath feels in your body, how it feels emotionally and what goes on in your head.

  Now repeat the exercise with a statement you know to be false and note how this feels on all levels. Make a note of the differences in your mind, body and heart when you repeat something true in comparison to something false.

- Start to get conscious about the information you receive and seek out; notice the times you turn outwards to seek information and try to make a conscious effort to pause before you do that – is this something you need to look elsewhere for or is it simply a force of habit not to trust yourself? Notice the way your mind, body and heart react to the various sources of information that come to you; are there particular sources that feel unpleasant or untrue?

Can you cultivate the information you receive so that it feels good, without placing yourself into too much of an echo chamber?

- As you work to find those places of your own truth, consider journeying with the core values that underpin your view of the world. Head to my website at **www.divinefeminist.com/ book** to download a worksheet which will lead you through the process of identifying and working with those values.

JOURNAL PROMPTS

- What is true to you, and how do you know that to be the case?

- What is untrue to you, and how do you know that to be the case?

- Where are the places that you feel more information to move forwards? Ask yourself why this is? Is that really true or are you holding yourself back?

COMMUNITY

INDIVDUAL   COLLECTIVE

We live in such individualistic societies, ones that pits us against each other in some sort of continual competition for power and respect in a way that at best drives personal insecurity and at worst leads to oppression and abuse.

There are so many examples of conflict and oppression that could be listed here, but in a book whose title includes the word "feminist" I want to write a little about the competition that is so often encouraged and ignited between women. We see it in the newspapers and magazines that report critically on the lifestyle and choices of any woman in the public eye, rather than on men in the same positions and we see it in our own daily lives where so many of us carry wounding from schoolgirl bullying and relationships and it is common knowledge that any group of women can be "so bitchy."

We're often told this sense of competition is rooted in the witch trials of the Middle Ages but to suggest that, tells only half the story; missing out so much of what went before and so much of what has come since.

It's no secret that humans were once a much more communally based species. Yuval Noah Harari's book *Sapiens* is a journey through the history of humankind as we know it so far, but one that really backed up my sadness over how disconnected we have become from ourselves and each other over time.

How does this topic link to the idea of rebalancing our world from those outwardly-facing solar energies to the more cyclical, often inward facing energies of the Moon? Simple, because individualism is a product of the societies that are so rooted in that imbalance and one that demands us to be always focussed, continually on our guard, and never able to truly pause and return to ourselves.

Once upon a time collectivism was the norm. We had no idea of "survival of the fittest" – a term that was coined by those looking for ways to assert dominance and has almost certainly been twisted further and promoted by those who were and are afraid of our power in numbers.

Out in the wild an individual – no matter how strong or clever – is only ever as safe as their worst day. An ailment, injury or bad night's sleep affects your reflexes? Then you are inevitably vulnerable – to the elements, predators or germs. And while that might be bearable for some species, we humans can find ourselves pretty far down the natural food chain at the best of times.

Together though, things change. We can leave the hunting and gathering to those who are up to it, while those who aren't as suited to that role can do something equally important, which fits their skills and abilities.

I am no historian and many of the societies I have glimpsed in readings and past life flashbacks are yet to be found by archaeologists. But those societies – the ones where things worked well – all had one thing in common: they involved us playing to our own individual strengths while working together in organic collectives within which everyone had their part.

What went wrong? Oh so many things. A drive for the kind of power that disagreed with that unity; the kind of power that couldn't be fed by the natural balance of the world, and by humanity as it was then. One of the first past life memories I had was of the fall of Atlantis. Long before I had read a book or watched a documentary on the subject, I dreamed of a beautiful place where people seemed largely content, cared for one another and the planet in a way that nurtured and respected everything and everyone for exactly who and what it was, almost regardless of what we brought to the table.

Change came with the idea that one thing was somehow better or worthier than another. Did desire for separation force that new mindset, or did the mindset of competition lead to a desire for separation? Honestly I don't know, it's one I have been trying to figure out ever since. But I do know the separation that followed made us weaker, not stronger, and led directly to the fall of that beautiful place and way of life.

Individualism is good for business

After all, how much money is spent by those trying to keep up with – or exceed – the Joneses and make sure they stand out from the crowd as the most attractive, stylish, cool? Individualism breeds insecurity as we do everything we can to try to stand out from the crowd. Or maybe insecurity breeds individualism as we approach everything in the world from that place of unsafety in our most primal needs, leading us to do everything we can to make ourselves safe by proving that we are worthy of not only acceptance but survival. That might sound a touch dramatic but let me explain why I say that.

Before training to be a therapist, I studied PR and built what could have been a successful career in corporate communications. You would think the two things were completely different but in reality both studies covered many of the same topics and theories. That sounds weird... until you learn that public relations was the brainchild of Edward Bernays, the nephew of one Sigmund Freud. Looking for ways to encourage the kind of behavioural changes his big money business and political clients wanted to see from the public, Bernays dove into his uncle's studies and theories and used them not to resolve people's inner conflicts, but to find ways to persuade people to look outside of themselves for those resolutions through actions they took and products they bought.

We still see evidence of this today in the advertisements that sell us products not by telling us what they actually do, but by showing us the ways in which those products could allegedly meet our needs by helping us climb a ladder to what Abraham Maslow called "self-actualisation." Think about the car adverts that focus not on how safely their vehicle will get us from A to B but on the beautiful, well-behaved families that drive happily through stunning, peaceful landscapes; and about the soft drink campaigns that say little about taste but instead show groups of oh-so-popular, cool people having the time of their lives while drinking a particular brand. It's pretty clever when you consider it, to suggest that a single can of liquid will give us the social status so many of us crave, but it's also not what Maslow, Freud or any of those early psychologists set out to do with their work.

This is undoubtedly why Freud eventually fell out with his nephew after Bernays encouraged him to "succeed" by focusing his work on the spread of government propaganda rather than the support of individual clients; and who can blame him? For all of his faults, Freud had ultimately been trying to help people, while Bernays had redirected that help towards companies and institutions who could use knowledge of our inner psychological workings as a tool for manipulation.

And manipulation is the word here. After all, turning to the Hierarchy of Needs theory that first led to the idea of self-actualisation, Maslow suggested that although everyone *could* reach the point he considered personal fulfilment and expansion, not everyone *will*. This is never more the case than in oppressed groups of people, who are encouraged to fight against one another in order to climb the rungs of a hierarchy where there simply wasn't enough space to go around.

I once heard a talk by Dr Shay-Akil McLean, in which he spoke about a group of slaves in 18th century North America who were threatening to rebel against their poor treatment, bad conditions and the horrors of slavery. When the slave owner caught wind of their plans, he had a brainwave. He took the white Irish slaves to one side – let's not forget this was a time when the Irish were considered to be lower than low – and told them that from this point forward they would be given more power and responsibility. After all, he told them, that was only fair since he knew white slaves were harder working, more reliable and worthier of power than their Black counterparts.

In an ideal world the Irish slaves would have recognised this for what it was and continued to see themselves as in community with, rather than competition against their Black friends. But as we know only too well, that's not what happened. In the short term it broke up their plans for rebellion – divided people have much less capacity for power after all; but in the longer term those divisive tactics undoubtedly had a part to play in the systematic racism we see so much of today.

Of course, division between people goes back further than the 18th century slave trade or the European witch trials. And as the racism, sexism, homophobia, transphobia, ableism and classism we see so much of today prove, it unfortunately doesn't end there. But to even consider truly resolving any of these things, we must go deeper than the boxes we have all been told divide us and the battle for safety we have all been told we must fight in.

Divided, we are weaker and easier to control. And while the seeds of those divisions go back deeper than our living memory, so deep that it is almost impossible to understand them, that doesn't mean they cannot be changed.

That is not to say that we should never strive for our own personal fulfilment, or give our all in this world of ours. Each of us have our own skills, talents and abilities and it is foolish and in many ways disrespectful to suggest we should tuck those talents away and refuse to shine our own light for fear of standing out from the crowd.

As some of my favourite ever words say in Marianne Williamson's A Return to Love:

"Your playing small does not serve the world. There is nothing enlightened about shrinking so that other people won't feel insecure around you. We are all meant to shine, as children do. We were born to make manifest the glory... that is within us. It's not just in some of us; it's in everyone. And as we let our own light shine, we unconsciously give other people permission to do the same. As we are liberated from our own fear, our presence automatically liberates others."

We support and work on ourselves because we deserve to be fulfilled, yes. But the best way to find that fulfilment is by shining those unique lights of ours out into the world in service of something greater than ourselves, in service of the collective need for everyone to be fulfilled and shining their lights.

We cannot do that without meeting our own needs. We cannot do that without stepping up to stand in the individual power and truth of that light and what it means to us. The difference here though lies in the intention; in whether we come from a place of personal gratification that asks us to stand above everyone else we meet, or one that invites us to stand shoulder to shoulder with the rest of the world as they do the same.

Should we all be one big happy family?

We've been told that's not the case; told that the differences between us are a threat and that the only way to be truly safe is to ensure that we protect only those who look like us. And once upon a time that may have been true. Hell, I live less than ten miles from a wall that is nearly 1,900 years old and was built specifically to keep out those who threatened to overthrow the colonising forces and reclaim the land they called home.

But even their battles were built on such bullshit. Isn't it time we begin to realise that the divisions we have been told about ourselves and each other are, so often, lies?

That while there are biological differences between humans, gender is no more than a performance which expresses itself differently in each culture and age?

That race isn't a truly biological factor – as Rachel Cargle's *The Great Unlearn* taught me, all humans have 99.9% of the same DNA, and you will find more genetic differences within racial groups than between them. Race is a societal construct established simply to segregate and classify people.

That, long before heterosexuality was considered the norm, bisexuality, pansexuality and homosexuality were just as widely accepted in many societies.

That the idea of neurotypicality we have been sold is based on outdated studies run on and by such a limited group of people that there is no way they can ever be imposed upon on the whole of humanity as the standard ways in which we "should" think or behave.

That geographic boundaries between countries, states and regions are no more than political lines drawn and redrawn multiple times throughout the history of Earth depending on who was in power and what their intentions were for the land.

That the amount of education someone has, money they call their own or home they do or don't live in doesn't make a person more or less than any other.

And that, if we can only unpick the stories that surround them, we will find almost every religion in the world began with the same basic principles; those of love and unity.

Yet how many lives have been lost over these things? How many people have been – and still are – enslaved, brutalised or murdered because someone somewhere believed that the differences between them made that group somehow less than their own? And how many wars have been fought because people and institutions were so heavily focussed on those differences that they were unable to respect another group or look for the similarities underneath?

I know, I'm over-simplifying. I am breaking down centuries of sociological, political and religious discourse into a matter of paragraphs that may sound unintentionally dismissive – especially coming from an educated, white, able bodied and cisgender woman. For that I apologise, and encourage you to look deeper into all of these subjects; the Resources section at the back of this book includes details of the work of some of my favourite leaders from the BIPOC, LGBTQIA+ and Disabled communities as a start.

But the point I am making is this: that embracing our similarities and honouring and respecting our differences within a global community is vital.

That's not an "all lives matter" statement, nor a glib dismissal of the things that differentiate us from one another which is where so much of the talk about us creating some sort of global collective makes me a little uneasy. The Merriam-Webster dictionary defines the word collective in a number of ways, the first as "denoting a number of persons or things considered as one group or whole." While yes, we are all humans living on planet Earth, all a part of the overall planetary ecosystem, to think of us all as one group can seem trite at best or offensive and triggering at worst.

Because of course every life matters, but when Black people and others from marginalised communities are penalised for simply existing, where Trans people are more likely to be murdered than cis, where Disabled people have nowhere near the same opportunities as able-bodied people, the playing field must be levelled and changes must be made before we can truly begin to talk about that. And until we reach a point where every person is safe and free to live wholly as themselves and have full access to the right opportunities for them, we must focus on the lives some people seem to see as dispensable.

There is no denying that we and our planet will benefit massively when we break down the bullshit behind the boxes that we have been placed into and begin to see and embrace one another as part of this same human species of ours. But the way to do that is not by trying to erase our differences and see us all as being the same.

Not only do our differences comprise so much of our beauty and our strength, but by ignoring those differences, we risk perpetuating so many of the inequities that cause so many problems in our societies today. We will never support one another to thrive, unless we acknowledge that none of us are the same.

That acknowledgement though, requires us to turn inwards just as much as it does to learn about and understand the broader world outside of ourselves. It means taking the time to unpack the judgments we carry about other people and the world, so that we can start to approach other people from a place of equity, even if the rest of the world isn't ready to do the same. When we think about any of the divisions in our society, it's so easy to look at those people at the far end of a spectrum and call them out as the problem. And yes, Neo Nazis, out and out misogynists and those churchgoers who like to wave abusive placards outside reproductive health centres and gay bars are *definitely* problematic to say the least. But their overt problems do not excuse us from the judgment and prejudices we carry within ourselves, consciously or otherwise as members of a society that is built upon so much of both.

We can't change what we have internalised and carried forwards to this point – any of us – but we can make a choice around what we do with that moving forwards, and how we unpack and heal those things in order to do as little damage as possible with them.

Then there are the ways in which our very existence in those structures of prejudice have benefited us personally, because turning inwards to do this work also requires us to pause and recognise our own privileges, and acknowledge the ways in which the current power structures of society benefit us personally. I know, that word "privilege" might just make you roll your eyes – I confess that it did me when I first heard it. As a working class woman growing up in one of the (at the time) poorest areas of the country with an accent that I've been told at various times makes me sound "stupid," "impossible to understand" and – my personal favourite – "unwashed and uneducated," the first time I was confronted with the idea of myself as privileged I found myself getting really angry. How dare they? Did the person suggesting that think I'd had it easy?!

So let me dispel that myth right away. By saying that you benefit from privilege, no-one is suggesting that you have had some sort of gold-paved pathway through life with never a challenge or a struggle to face. None of us have that – even those who have the odds of society stacked firmly in their favour. But it does mean that there is some area of society where you have benefitted simply by the nature of your background or how you appear in the world.

Take me as an prime example; I am a woman who has experienced sexism in various forms; I am working class in a society built by and for the financially prosperous; a Northern person in a country where many, even today, seem to see the area "north of the wall" (or London) in the same way they do in Game of Thrones; and have an accent that still makes people from other parts of the country switch off from any serious attempts at discussion, as soon as I open my mouth.

However, I am also a white woman in a society built upon white supremacy and colonialism; I am cisgender meaning I have never had to fight to live life as the person I know myself to be; every romantic relationship in my life has been heterosexual, meaning that I have never had to fear abuse or violence as I walked down a street hand in hand with the person I loved; my physical and mental abilities mean I have been able to move through life without significant obstacles in those areas; I have had access to literacy and education; I have a roof over my head and come from a loving, stable family, who I know will always support me. While my privileges do not negate the ways that I have experienced oppression, they do outweigh them, and mean that I have also – inadvertently or otherwise been what Rachel Ricketts calls an "oppressed oppressor."

Rachel's book Do Better is a must read on this subject which, as a white woman, I am not qualified to write about in detail, but I do seriously encourage you to really confront the uncomfortable and do the work to understand and unpack your own privileges and how an acceptance of and participation in those has contributed to you, like me, upholding the systems of oppression that so badly need to be overturned.

If and when we can all break down those internal prejudices and begin to use our own places of privilege for the benefit of others, then maybe we will have the very first foundations upon which to create a global community where we can all truly feel and believe that we are part of something bigger through which we serve one another and this planet we call home. But that community must always be one that honours our differences just as much as our similarities.

Humans as part of the whole

One of the easiest ways to explain the ways in which we all co-exist with one another within this world is as part of an ecosystem; an interconnected network of beings who all – knowingly or otherwise – support and rely upon one another as they play their own role within that wider network.

All members of an ecosystem have similarities – in our case the fact that we are all members of the same species, on the same planet – but also have their own unique part to play within that ecosystem in order to somehow support one another and the rest of our planet to thrive. No one person or group of people is responsible for the overall ecosystem or has answers on how it can work best; but we do all have our own roles to play both in supporting one another and in doing our own thing.

To honour that ecosystem, we must honour all of our differences and celebrate the beauty, wisdom and power such diversity brings and the different ways in which each of those benefit our species and our planet. We must recognise that none of us have all of the answers, but in the fullness of witnessing and respecting one another's experiences and wisdom, we might just all find some solutions and some roads forward – something that is so desperately needed right now.

For all of those things to happen we must find a way to create safe and supportive spaces for everyone on Earth to be themselves, and do the work needed to break down the divisions within them in order that we can break down the divisions that are keeping so many of us at war. That's challenging. Hell, as I write this I would even go so far as to call it terrifying. After all, it is extreme differences of opinion – both historically in the creation of power structures and belief systems that underpin our societies and today in every aspect of our societies – that have led to the abuse and persecution of so many.

So how do we overcome that? How can we ever see ourselves as connected to those whose viewpoints can feel dismissive, disrespectful or even life-threatening? There is no easy way, no magic pill that will suddenly help those at the far end of a spectrum see how terrifying and unreasonable their views seem to another person, but the journey always starts with two things; education and empathy.

It involves us going out to learn about the world, educating and informing ourselves enough that our fears – because let us remember that all prejudice starts with an element of fear – become less terrifying and the dark corners of our own judgments are illuminated with truth and understanding.

It's easy to see the recent rise in activism as a product of profile raising by the many campaigns on social media and the fact that injustices can no longer be carried out behind the scenes of our world where no-one will ever find out. And maybe there is some truth to that. But I also think the increasing drive for activism in our society is down to increasing numbers of people becoming more community-minded; doing the work on themselves that sees them step into their role as part of a broader collective that needs them to show up and do the work – not only in their own interests but also in the interests of those around them.

That's not to say that we should sacrifice ourselves for the collective, no. Of course we must step out of our places of comfort and often speak up or act out in ways that challenge us and bring a threat of persecution or criticism. Taking on a role of activist even in the smallest ways will require that. But it doesn't have to require losing yourself completely; in fact often activism involves playing to your strengths – using those skills, gifts and yes, privileges that you have in the service of something greater than yourself be that by giving your time or money, by marching, by writing or speaking, by educating, by supporting other activists or by some awesome combination of all of the above. Our pursuit of change and our role in the breaking down of divisions will inevitably look different to someone else's, but as long as we are taking genuine action, that does not make it more or less valid than anyone else's.

We all have privileges and past shames to unpack and of course we must work through, challenge and overcome those. But we must also remember that we can't do those things if we're exhausted and broken.

There must be a balance. There must always be a balance because the stakes are high, and not only for us humans.

Because let us be clear; the divided and individualistic way we humans are living our lives right now is not just damaging us as a species, it is damaging the whole of our world and every species that belongs to this planetary ecosystem we are a part of. We have worked so hard to become bigger, better and more powerful that we have spread ourselves and the footprint of our species far beyond the place that was allotted to us on this ecosystem. As someone who practices a nature-based belief system maybe I'm a little biased, but recognising ourselves as part of a global community also means recognising the broader community that planet is home to and coming back to a place of seeing ourselves within, rather than separate from, or above that community. In *The Dream of the Earth,* ecopsychologist Thomas Berry said: "Our challenge is to create a new language, even a new sense of what it is to be human. It is to transcend not only national limitations, but even our species isolation, to enter into the larger community of living species. This brings about a completely new sense of reality and value."

The Fourth Key: EMPATHY

And this is where empathy comes into play, something that is vital whenever we create a safe space.

In my first counselling class, I remember being told about Carl Rogers' core conditions of empathy, authenticity and unconditional personal regard, the three things he believed create a safe space in which people can change and grow. After describing those to us, the tutor asked if there was anything a client could bring to a session that we wouldn't be able to have empathy for.

That first list of mine was pretty long, but the more I trained and the more I came to understand about myself and other people, the more I began to recognise it wasn't quite so simple. Everyone is carrying their own wounds, fears and shames, and so often it is those things, rather than some innate evil, which drive us into places of anger and to the actions that hurt or demean other people.

Of course, you may not be a therapist in the business of providing a safe space for everyone you meet, so you don't have to reach exactly the same place. But that doesn't mean you can't, as my tutor used to say, walk a mile in another person's shoes, just as long as you remember to keep your own socks on along the way.

That means staying true to ourselves. This journey will lead you to get angry and frustrated with other people's viewpoints. At times it will trigger your own wounding and leave you wanting to retreat into a cave as far as possible from the rest of the human race and in those moments it is vital that we take the time and support to get ourselves through that safely.

To empathise does not mean we have to forgive everyone – or anyone – or condone their behaviour. And it doesn't require us to overstep our own boundaries or put ourselves in danger of any sort. It also doesn't mean we can never challenge another person's viewpoint or that we should refrain from sharing our own or standing up for what we believe in.

But it does mean to recognise one another as human. Scared and often wounded people who are just trying to get ourselves through life in the safest ways possible, often without stopping to consider the ways our beliefs and actions impact upon other people.

Valarie Kaur's *See No Stranger* is one of the most powerful books I have ever read. In that book, Valarie tells the stories of the Sikh American community in the years since 9-11, and leads a call for revolutionary love – something she calls the "choice to enter into labour for others who do not look like us, the opponents who hurt us, and for ourselves," as she explains that all three forms of love are equally vital. Valarie writes of the Sikh warrior saints and the ways that, when we hear the stories of others, we cannot help but see those others as people and to feel a connection to them.

You would think the greatest challenge of adopting an empathetic approach to humanity would be this aspect; being asked to empathise with a person whose view of the world you fundamentally disagree with, or maybe even to look inside of yourself and face up to your own internalised prejudice and shame. Yes, both of those things are definitely tough.

But there is another part of this key that makes it one of the most challenging in this book; that when we truly embrace empathy and recognise ourselves and each other as part of the same community, the depth of feeling that arises is enough to make the idea of walking away or numbing more than a little tempting. It is easy to see that as a weakness, but that is not the case.

Empathy is a strength. Empathy is always a strength.

To feel deeply – not just your own feelings, but also those of others – is one of the greatest superpowers of our humanity because it forces us to see the world differently. In a way, that reminds us we are all connected, and we are all worthy of a safe space to tend our wounds.

And that means giving ourselves a place to tend wounds too; recognising that the shadows, pains, fears and griefs that will come up as we work through this will be tough, and giving ourselves the space and the nurturing we need to work through that process, not because we are selfish or hiding from outward action, but because we recognise it is an important part of enabling our outward action.

EXERCISES AND PROMPTS

MEDITATION

Connecting to the world: Together we will journey to the tree at the Heart of Gaia to plug back into the network of Earth to which she connects.

RITUAL

Honouring yourself: What could be more powerful than to carry out a ritual in the name of yourself? Gather together the things that bring pleasure to your senses, and join me in a ritual carried out purely to honour yourself.

Honouring someone else: This one needs a few less props, but is no less powerful, enabling you to honour another person who is important to you without in any way impinging on their freewill.

EXERCISES

- Take a day to consciously notice the judgements you make about people and situations as you move through the world. What do you automatically think about and/or feel around someone because of how they look or who they are? Keep a note throughout the day and once you get home journal on this – where do these beliefs and ideas come from?

- Taking this one step further the following day, what if you were to approach everyone you meet from a place of empathy; wondering each and every time you are tempted to judge what were the stories that had led this person to the action or belief system you are tempted to be critical of? How does that change the ways in which you see other people and the world?

- Thinking about the ways you occupy a place of privilege in the world, how can you use that position for good? Where can you take affirmative action to drive change?

- Remember one of the most important factors in changing the world is to care for ourselves and our own pains. How will you nurture and have empathy for yourself first and foremost on this journey?

JOURNAL PROMPTS

- What are your safe spaces and the communities you feel you belong to?

- What couldn't you hold space for?

- What makes you feel safe and accepted?

- How do and can you do good?

- Where and how could you do more?

- Where are your places of privilege, and where are your places of oppression?

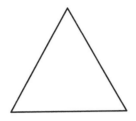

fire

The spark of creation, luminator of paths and incubator of new beginnings.

Fire is the passion that forces us to demand change, that blazes a trail out of the dark ages and into a new dawn of greater enlightenment.

It is the warmth of a candle when our hands are cold from digging through shadows, and the alchemical flame with the power to transform all.

We welcome it in the South with the heat of the midday Sun, the enchanting days of Summer and the fertility of the Mother.

In Summer we find the Soul; with the heat of its certainty and the strength to discern.

With Fire comes the first fires of the morning as each new day dawns.

And with Fire comes the last embers of the setting sun, burning away what is no longer needed, as we surrender into the dark.

To forget Fire is to be cold and empty of drive or passion. It is to be without the ignition needed to ever move forwards.

To restrict Fire is to consign another to the darkness, left to wander aimlessly with no view of what lies ahead.

But to leave Fire untended is to risk the whole world catching ablaze; a world ruled by tempers and passion unwilling to pause.

It is to follow the callings of passion without ever stopping to consider their effect on the world around us or even the entirety of our own beings.

But Fire is enlightenment, truth and the first spark of all that is new. It deserves to live in balance.

And so we call to the South, and to Fire. To the height of the Sun to the Mother, the Summer and to the Fullness of the Moon.

We call to the dragons and the phoenixes, to the volcanoes and their lava, to the salamanders that breathe and walk in the flames.

And we ask them to join, to work with us and to bless us with their warmth, their sparks and their illumination as we continue our journey towards true rebalancing.

To Fire and the South, hail and welcome.

May it be so.

To hear this invocation in full along with a short story, **The Dragons Beneath the Land,** visit the additional materials link at the back of the book.

SELF-KNOWING

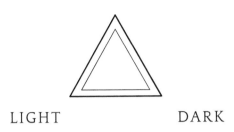

LIGHT   DARK

If I had a pound for every time I had heard or read the words "love and light" then I would be a very rich woman.

As we've mentioned previously there is nothing wrong with love – after all as a wise man once said, it's the one thing that there's just too little of. And equally there is nothing wrong with light. It's something we all need to grow and to survive. But as with so many outwardly positive terms, this is a sentiment that has been hugely weaponised over recent years. Because make no mistake, a world that was only love and light would not be a world in balance.

I understand where this has come from, of course. We have long been told to fear the dark and any emotions that are "less than" love. And no wonder, those are scary places where our fears, shames and shadows are lying in wait for us.

But the darkness also holds a great deal of power – a power we need if we are ever going to rebalance our own lives and the wider world.

In the beginning, there was darkness

Before the Big Bang created our Universe and before each of us emerged from the birth canal screaming at the sudden bright lights, loud noises and less than perfect temperatures, darkness was our natural home. Yet it is the thing so many of us are afraid of.

It's easy to put that fear down to the lack of light. As creatures without perfect night vision, who thrive on the light and the warmth of the Sun, we spend our time in the dark waiting to be pounced upon by all manner of terrifying things that go bump in the night.

But the more time I spend in the darkness, the more I come to realise that the scariest thing about it isn't the lack of light or anything else, but the inclusion of everything...

In the darkness anything and everything seems both possible and close enough to touch; not only the things we want to see and hear about, but also those we do such a good job of keeping at bay during the daylight hours. The darkness is the place of potential, and maybe because of that it's absolutely terrifying to we humans who find comfort in certainty and safety, not to mention that the world has conditioned us to be that way.

I began formally practicing as a medium in my early 20s, but have seen and felt spirit for as long as I can remember. My parents tell a great story about a two or three year old me walking through a British seaside town chattering away to someone no-one else could see. And while other people looked questioningly at me, my parents just nodded and waved with an air of, "Yes, we know. This is absolutely normal in our lives."

Having seen and heard things other people couldn't for most of my life, I spent a long time being afraid of the dark, and more specifically of what I would see without the bright, distracting lights of day. Whenever I woke up through the night, I'd squeeze my eyes closed so tightly they hurt, and clutch my pillow over my ears as though it was protecting me from certain death (I've always been just a tad dramatic). Even as an adult, waking up in the middle of the night involved squeezing my eyes shut as I groped for every light switch between my bed and wherever I needed to be.

I had done these things for so long they seemed natural, until I started to work with my own subconscious and realised that maybe it had never been spirit visitors I was afraid of.

That work required me to get still and quiet, away from the noise and bright lights of the day. And whenever that happened, I would immediately be faced with the shame, insecurities, anxieties and guilt that wanted to be witnessed – something more terrifying than any spirit I am yet to meet. It turns out that my key to getting comfortable in the darkness involved sitting with that until each of those things became so familiar that they no longer had any power over me. I learned to stay rooted into myself and the truth of who I am, no matter how much those voices from the shadows may whisper and shout, rather than trying desperately to turn away from the parts of myself that weren't so welcome, in a desperate search for the light.

It sounds terrifying I know. Who the hell wants to get cosy with their darkest moments?! Yet here's what I learned by doing exactly that; that the shadows within us are nowhere near as monstrous as I had expected, and that much like the fear we have spoken about before, sitting with them allowed me to get comfortable with everything those parts of me were truly trying to hide – awakening a deep sense of power as a result.

Once I learned to forgive myself for my perceived guilt, to have empathy for the wounds that had led to my most shameful actions, I started to see the powers they had been disconnecting me from.

The power of using my voice, once I stopped fearing that people would judge me – like the "friend" who had told me that her greatest nightmare was her son growing up to speak with an accent as common as mine.

The ways I could help other people by talking about, rather than hiding from, my own shame and regrettable experiences.

The truths that were waiting underneath the criticism and abuse other people had thrown at me to mask their own insecurities.

The fury that roared at me like a wild beast, but also propelled me into action on the causes that stirred my heart and soul.

And the peace that came when I no longer had to block out those noises or voices and could simply rest and breathe.

Not that this was an easy journey. It took years of journaling and a good couple of chunks of time in therapy. But the more I connected with the place of darkness within myself, the more I was able to clear out the less than fun companions I found there, and instead connect with the true beauty and power that lies in darkness.

Because there is an important factor in this that our light-focussed society has tried hard to disconnect us from: there is both power and beauty to be found in the dark.

When I began to claim the title of witch (more on that in the next chapter!) and follow the Celtic wheel of the year that is so sacred to nature-based belief systems in my culture, I realised that darkness wasn't always considered negative; in the days before electric lighting and heating, the coldest and darkest parts of our year were embraced just as much as the warmer, brighter months, with people gathering their animals, crops and families and heading indoors to hunker down for the winter. Imagine that! Hunkering down, rather than forcing ourselves out of bed to defrost the car on a cold, dark morning and staying in an office until long after sunset so we head to bed having barely glimpsed natural light throughout the day. I can't help but think there is a lot to be said for switching off and hibernating like so many of the animal kingdom are wise enough to do!

Not that winter months back then were wasted; those months of indoor time were used to rest, recoup their energies at the end of a busy year and reconnect, with their families, communities, ancestors and themselves.

One of the things that makes me saddest of all about the ways our society has become so solar-focussed is exactly that; the fact that we are never encouraged to truly step away from the world and rest in a way that allows us to return refreshed and with entirely new insights on the situations we are facing.

We consider the darkness in terms of a cave holding monsters and terrors, because that is exactly what we are sold through stories, movies and the fearful voices of our own shadows. But in doing that, we forget to consider just how much stillness, insight and peace can come from that space of germination that lives below the Earth, and of how much wisdom can be found when we connect with the wise crone who lives in the darkest of the caves.

Last Samhain I decided it was time to conquer my fear of the dark once and for all. As part of my ritual to celebrate the holy day, I ventured into the (very safe, with people no more than five minutes' away and nothing likely to eat me) woods alone.

They were woods I'd walked into at least 100 times before, but heading in that night with the shadowy trees obscuring even the light of the stars and moon, the darkness was as thick as a blanket and I felt that old terror returning as loudly as the pounding of my heart in my chest.

As I walked I repeated the Terry Pratchett quote: "A witch ought never to be frightened in the darkest forest... because she should be sure in her soul that the most terrifying thing in the forest was her." Over and over again I said it in my head, reminding myself that whatever I saw, whatever the woods held for me, I absolutely had the power to match it.

I sat down on a fallen tree a little way in, looking out at the lake in front of me and closed my eyes, allowing myself to feel into the energy of the forest around me as I called in the elements and cast my own mental circle of protection. I remember immediately there was a gust of wind that whipped my hair around my face – shit got serious and the old, scared part of me wanted to get up and run back to the lodge.

But there I was, in my witch circle on Halloween, telling myself a witch need never be afraid in the darkest forest... So I stayed. Stayed as I heard the shuffles and whispers of nature around me, as I felt spirit sit next to me and put hands on my shoulders, and even as some of my greatest insecurities shouted loudly to make themselves heard.

Yet amongst all of that, I realised there really wasn't anything to be afraid of; that in reality it had never been any of those things I was afraid of, but the inner belief that maybe I wasn't powerful enough to face any of them. A not-enoughness that went deeper than how I looked, what the other kids thought of me or how much money I had in the bank.

When it came time to leave the forest I decided to challenge that underlying fear and walked back out with my eyes closed. Yup, since my eyes had become just accustomed enough to see shapes in the darkness, I decided it was time to take even that away and walk back along the path blind. I walked slowly and carefully at first, more aware than ever of the way the path felt below my feet and of the surroundings I could sense around me. Admittedly, it turns out I can't trust my senses quite so well when I can't see, given that the one time a giant gust of wind forced me to open my eyes, I found myself having veered off the path and face to face with a giant pointy tree! However, I did reconcile myself with the fact that the wind had come to save me, and fairly danced back to the cabin, feeling a bit like the Northumbrian forest's answer to Moana as I laughed at the fact that maybe I did need just a little bit of light after all!

The power of the light

And make no mistake, we all need light. Just ask those people who live in the most northerly parts of Iceland where the Sun only rises for two hours on the shortest day of the year. It is no coincidence that rates of depression and anxiety tend to rise in the Winter months and we all know the many vitamins and minerals our human bodies need that come from the Sun.

That star is one of the main life forces of our planet and the centre of our solar system for a reason. So is it any surprise that, despite its archetypal connections to the Moon, even those things considered to be a reclamation of the Divine Feminine have tried to avoid the darkness?

That focus on love and light may well link into the gentle, nourishing and beauty-filled archetypes of the Mother and the Full Moon that we are all so familiar with. And the Goddess practitioners who wear beautiful pink kaftans and speak solely about joy and beauty are undoubtedly tapping into some seriously important energies. Hell, pink may not be my colour but those energies are things we tap into in this book too, and for good reason.

The word "lightworker" is used a lot in the spiritual fields, and in honesty one I personally can't stand, because it can lead you to believe that any work we do in service of changing the world must always be bright, shiny and positive. This work – the work of getting to know yourself so that you can truly make a difference in the world as the fullest version of yourself – can be fun and sparkly and shiny yes, but often it is far from that. Often the light comes only after we have dived into the darkest depths of our experiences and the experiences of others so that we can retrieve the missing pieces that help bring the overall bigger picture puzzle of someone's journey here to life. Often the lights we shine are on the things that other people would prefer were kept hidden, so as not to upset their comfortable balance of power within this world and everything we do. And then it is time to shine a light on something we find more uncomfortable rather than sparkly; bright and hot enough to make those things we've long consigned to the darkness recoil back in horror and maybe even attack more ferociously as they fight their way back to something safe.

As I learned on my journey into the woods, light changes the way we see things, but that doesn't always mean those things are suddenly shiny and welcoming. Sometimes bringing ourselves and our fullness into the light can show up a new dimension of shame and horror at what we have been dealing with.

But that's not to say that everything needs to be out there under the beams of sunlight every single moment of every day. We can choose which parts of ourselves we shine a light upon at any given moment, in order to allow ourselves the time and the space to reconnect with those parts that need a little more tending before they can be made public. This is where we come back to the cyclical energies of the Moon; because the lunar cycle doesn't begin with the bright fullness we all hear so much about, or even with the first slivers of newness we are so regularly told are our opportunity to set intentions for the month ahead; it begins in a place of complete darkness, as the Moon comes back slowly but surely into a place of its own fullness before retreating back into the shadows again. And often this is the case with the parts of ourselves and our world that need to be worked with in order to make change.

We begin with the hard and challenging work of bringing those things out of the darkness; setting intentions as we begin our journey for what it is that we are truly looking to do and change. More and more, we shine a light on our findings, until they are well and truly illuminated and we can see them for what they are. And right there, in the light of their fullness, we are able to see what can be taken forwards and what it is time to leave behind once and for all; giving that which is no longer useful to us back into the grave of darkness where its remnants can transmute into useful wisdom or insight.

As you would expect, this is never something we do once and then walk away from. It is a continual process for ourselves, and for the world around us, of understanding what needs to be brought out of the shadows into the light, what can stay in the darkness to rest and grow and what can be discarded once and for all, each time we move through the process of change.

There is no denying that many things – us included – thrive in the light, and that a part of what that term "lightworker" refers to is the drive for each of us to do our own thing in a way that recognises us as worthy of that thriving and allows us to be seen in the fullness of who we are. After years, generations and lifetimes of persecution and abuse for living and expressing ourselves in the wholeness of who we are that can often feel even more terrifying than to stay amongst the shadows, but that's not to say that it should be avoided.

We change this world so that we can all enjoy the light on our faces for exactly who and what we are. And where that means those of us who would be more comfortable tucking ourselves away in the dark stepping into the spotlight of centre stage, we take a big breath, work ourselves through the cycle of integration, surround ourselves with the people who will support every step of the journey. And then shine that damned light, knowing that we are worthy of it.

And in doing so, we remember the power in each of us as lighthouses – shining the kind of lights that assure other people they are not alone, and letting them know just where to head for safe harbour as they weave their own way through that same process of retrieving what is needed from the darkness.

Owning the shadow and the shine

The key to all of this; both to navigating our own light and shadows and to understanding which of our shadows need to step into the light, and which of our shiniest areas need to be consigned to the darkness, is to get to know ourselves fully.

That's not just about solo date days doing something fun, nor about knowing which outfits make us feel most confident and at home in ourselves (although both of those things are important too). It's about the kind of deep self-knowledge that allows us to recognise and own every single part of ourselves.

It's about owning our shit as much as we do our brightness and about befriending the pieces of ourselves we are most afraid to show to the world, just as much as those we are wholly comfortable to share. And why wouldn't we? You are the only person you will be with for every single moment of your life; why isn't that a relationship you should cultivate?

But that's not always easy. Our connection to self is something that has been so badly damaged over the years, with so many of us being told that inner connection is indulgent and "selfish" rather than something that not only helps us move through life more smoothly, but also helps us to be more of service in the ways in which we work and move in the world. Overcoming those messages can make the process of sitting down to reconnect with ourselves seem difficult to the point of impossible. But so often it begins with the simple choice to sit down with a pen and ask, "What do I need to know?" Before writing everything that comes to mind.

Of course, as a therapist, I believe that personal therapy is an important step on the road to...well, anything I guess! But in this case, I cannot stress how beneficial it can be to have a safe and impartial space to sort through your own stuff and cultivate the kind of deep knowledge and understanding of ourselves that allows us to recognise our own wisdom, as well as the shadows and blockages that we carry within, and those we are inadvertently projecting out into the world around us.

There are multiple times in my life that a therapist has helped me to step back from the unhelpful thought or behaviour patterns I had fallen into, by listening solely to what someone else had to say, or by ignoring a vital piece of information because some hidden part of me didn't want it to be true. And equally, I think of the times I have offered that new perspective to a client and helped them to break through a barrier and get to know themselves in a new – and undoubtedly fuller – way as a result.

Cultivating our understanding of self doesn't just allow us to connect to the inner knowing we spoke of earlier, it also helps us to connect to that place of discernment that we already know is so important. A place where the external perspectives and agendas no longer lead us on a merry dance of deception, but instead help us to see what is truly right for us personally.

For me a good example is around motherhood. When I reached my mid-30s, I began to question if I really did want the children I had always dreamed of, or whether society had drummed this idea of motherhood into my head for so long that I could no longer discern its agenda from my heart's desires, something I had seen happen with so many other women of my generation. The idea of not having kids sounded uncomfortable to me, but then with my "biological clock" allegedly ticking (sigh, couldn't that be the subject of a whole other book? But I digress.) I was conscious of making a huge decision and potentially messing up the life of another person for reasons that really weren't my own.

How could I ever figure out which was the right path for me when both seemed pretty loud, dark and scary? The answer came in diving into the shadowy fears and shames of both sides of that argument; not only discerning the guilts and anxieties behind each voice but also taking the time to negotiate between the two. It came with sitting in that place of questioning how I felt about the idea of never having children and what would happen if that was my decision, and then with sitting in the place of certainty that I did want to have children before investigating all of the voices that spoke up as a result of both perspectives.

What came to light was a clear decision, but not packaged as the simple clear and shiny viewpoint I had expected. Instead it offered a whole cacophony of experiences, expectations, anxieties, wishes, shame, hopes and wisdom that helped me understand what I truly felt and needed.

For the record they showed me that yes, I do want to be a mother – be that biologically or otherwise – but that there are an awful lot of societal expectations I need to shake off and work through if I want to do that on the terms I feel would best enable me to support another human as they grow and learn in the world.

The Fifth Key: FAITH

The key to all of this – to acknowledging your darkness and your shine and to getting comfortable with both, is in one little word that is possibly one of the heaviest of our times: Faith.

You must have faith in yourself and the fullness of who you are, outside of what you have been told. The kind of self-belief that reminds us – even at the scariest of times – that we are more than what we have learned and experienced and more than what anyone else may have told us about ourselves.

I know, I see you rolling your eyes. Hey, as I write this midway through a fun visit from my own inner imposter, I feel my own eyes rolling, but it's true.

This society of ours has worked hard to keep us all so small; through the practical systems of oppression I have written about elsewhere, through the diminishing of concepts and ideas that represent the routes to so much of our power and through the people that have gone before us, that it is safer and easier to just stay small and quiet. But as I have undoubtedly written elsewhere in this book, a force will only work that hard to subdue its opposition when it believes that opposition to be a threat.

You are a threat to the systems of oppression that demand you to show up in the world in a specific, socially acceptable, Insta-perfect way. And when you take the time to cultivate the self-knowledge that allows you to connect to the fullness of yourself? Well then my friend you are unstoppable. Absofuckinglutely unstoppable.

And if you don't have the faith in that for yourself right now, then allow me to hold it for you. Or find a safe and supportive circle who will do that (if you don't know of one off the top of your head then check out the Divine Feminist community, a place designed for exactly that reason. You can find details of the community at **www.divinefeminist.com/community**).

To have faith in ourselves doesn't require us to have faith in every part of ourselves, or even to like every part of ourselves. All that is required to start is faith in one single thing – the time you stood up for something you believe in, the one place where you always feel safe and confident, or the one area of your life in which you always feel wholly and completely like you; that one thread of yourself that you know, intimately and have faith in within yourself. Remind yourself of that daily, hourly if you need to and let that one thing be the seed which allows a fuller bloom of faith in yourself to take root and flower.

EXERCISES AND PROMPTS

Please note that the exercises and prompts in this section may be tough. Please ensure you seek support as and where you need to and don't venture into the depths of your own shadows unless you feel safe to do so.

MEDITATIONS

Meet yourself in your wholeness: What would it be to meet yourself as you could and were always meant to be? On this short meditation we will journey inwards to meet you in your wholeness.

Getting to know your shadow: Shadow work is one of the most potent things we can do, although this meditation comes with a warning. Although you will be kept safe throughout, take this journey only when you feel grounded and comfortable to do so.

RITUAL

A ritual for self-forgiveness: So many of us carry guilt, shame and pain for things we have – or haven't – done in the past. This deep and powerful ritual will support you to forgive yourself for the burdens that you are carrying consciously or otherwise.

EXERCISES

- Spend some time – ideally on the night of the dark moon – alone in the darkness. Ensure you are physically safe, and then turn off the lights all except for maybe one candle and as you sit there in that place see what comes up for you and how it feels to sit in that space without light.

- Try standing in front of a mirror – for extra power do this without make-up or even without clothes – and look yourself straight in the eye. Again, pay attention to what comes up for you, as you do this. Practice this regularly if you can.

  Once you become more comfortable with simply standing in front of the mirror, try to repeat positive statements as you look yourself in the eye. Things like "I love you," and "All of you is welcome here," are great places to start, although also consider using this exercise to repeat all the ways you have faith in yourself and all of the positive things you know to be true about yourself.

JOURNAL PROMPTS

- What do you think of when you consider the idea of darkness?

- What about when you consider the idea of light and brightness?

- Take some time to write down all the labels you use to describe yourself; from the names other people call you, to the ways in which you describe yourself. Take the time to connect with each of those labels in turn and then turn a page and write who you are underneath them all?

- Make a list of everything you are proud of, everything you believe (or have been told) you are good at and everywhere you feel safe and confident. Keep this list somewhere safe and review it regularly to remember how bloody amazing you are.

- Elsewhere, make a list of everything you are less proud of – your shame, your pain and your guilt. List them all and then go through each one and ask yourself, truly, what led to this? Keep asking why, over and over again for each and every one of those, until you get to the root cause for each of these things. How does it feel to consider the whys behind these things?

- Where and how do you have faith in yourself?

WHOLENESS

POWER OVER   POWER WITHIN

I have spoken elsewhere in this book about my practice as a witch, and this is the chapter where we all get witchy, and to the root of the thing that our unbalanced world has been trying so damned hard to keep us from:

Power.

Some of us will scrunch our faces up at that word, and declare that power is something we don't and shouldn't want, maybe even something terrifying that we don't believe we can be trusted with.

I get it. The power we have been told about for most of living memory, in the media we consume and in pretty much the whole world around us, is unpleasant and scary in so many ways. Not to mention exclusive to the point that even having power seems unlikely unless we, our lives and our faces fit a very particular mould.

But the power I'm talking about is different. It is not one that is granted by society and sees us oppress other people in order to assert our dominance and get our own way. It is a power within us that allows us to truly grow and shine; one we don't need an epic quest to find, or some sort of bloody way to claim as our own, one that is there within us, stirring occasionally as it tries to make itself known to us but otherwise waiting patiently for us to reconnect with it.

Power as we know it

The power we are so familiar with is one that works for some people sure, but definitely not all of us. We can see that ourselves, simply by looking at the ways people across the world are discriminated against and cut off from opportunities, because they look a certain way, come from a particular background, or identify in a way that goes against the dominant structures of society.

I could give thousands of examples of that, and have given a few elsewhere in this book, but it is fair to say that if you are reading this book then you will be familiar with more than a few of those examples already. And with those many examples in mind, how can we ever consider the distribution of power to be fair or, as many countries claim, completely democratic?

There is no denying that the structures of power, which see some have power over others, can be awful and are, in almost all cases, terribly unbalanced. But they are also familiar to us. Familiar in a way that often makes us feel safe and believe them to be "natural." I remember watching a documentary about the fall of communism in the old Soviet Union and how, even before the economic and political structures of that society crumbled, people knew that they weren't working. The leaders knew some sort of crash was coming, but continued to pretend otherwise so as not to cause concern and lose their positions of power, while the majority of the population also knew something was terribly wrong, but were so ingrained into a particular way of thinking and living, that they were unable to see an alternative. So they also went about their business pretending everything was fine.

In many ways, that is how it is with the balance of power in many of our current Western societies. We know that so much is broken, and even when we step outside and begin to question, it can seem impossible to know where to start. So impossible, that many people either stop questioning and resign themselves to a future within a society that will never serve them, or buy into the kind of theories that promise a moment of reckoning in which "good" will win out over "bad" and the whole world will be reborn as a fair and beautiful society.

I understand those viewpoints. Hell, I have fallen victim to both in the past and with the memories I've mentioned which feature idyllic societies like Atlantis and pre-Babylon Mesopotamia, you might well think I belong to the latter group who are waiting for some race of truly democratic space beings to come along, click their glowing fingers and reset our whole society. In some ways, I'd bloody love that to be the case – it sounds way easier than the alternative!

But the truth is that any significant change takes work, hard work, from all of us. That only comes when we step back from everything we've been told is "normal" and "best" and start to question those things both to our benefit and to our detriment and then take action internally and externally. I have written elsewhere about the need to understand and unpack our own privilege and the many ways that we put our own power into action by using our voices, taking to the streets, refusing to participate in oppressive or non-representative projects, actively supporting causes related to, or artists and business owners from, under-represented communities and doing what we can to change the narratives of our communities; re-dressing the balance even when that change of balance doesn't seem to be in our favour at all.

Although spoiler: any rebalancing of power from the oppressive, hierarchical systems we currently experience into a place of true equity and fairness will always be in our favour. Will always be in the favour of all.

That, though, is where this gets sticky. Because when we have spent lifetimes being told that power is an exclusive force only a limited group of people have access to, we will – in a way understandably – cling on to the power we do have like some sort of lifebuoy in a sea of chaos. Especially when no-one can explain to us exactly what the alternative will look like, and how that will benefit us.

Right now, no-one can explain that largely none of us – even me writing this book that speaks of the need for sacred rebalance – know where that path will take us and exactly how it will look in the long run. But I do know where it starts: with each of us reconnecting with our own power.

You've always had the power my dear

"Whoa there," you might just be saying. *"I don't have a great deal of power. And even if I did, I'm not sure I could handle using it. Who's to say I wouldn't go all Thanos circa Avengers Infinity War and click away half the Universe given half the chance?"*

I hear you. And in some ways the power we have within us is scary. It is definitely something the people at the very top of the privilege scale are scared of. But the very process of remembering and connecting with our power is, if done properly, to move out of the wounds and insecurities that have passed that fear onto us.

There are a few things you should know about the power that lies within you. Firstly that it is both a generic part of being part of this world – we are all seriously fucking powerful, no matter what the outside world may have led us to believe – and something that is uniquely and potently you. Secondly that truly living and breathing it will never diminish another person, although it may just spark inspiration for them to live in their own place of power. It's like the old line about the candle that is able to light 100 others. You will never lose any of your own brightness by encouraging others to burn more brightly for themselves.

My favourite part of working with clients usually comes about halfway through our work together. It is the moment when a client, who has always been so burdened by the challenges of their past and weighed down by all of the ways the world has told them they aren't enough, logs into a session and just looks… different. Their shoulders look sturdier, their eyes brighter and they shine with a light that can only be described as totally and utterly them.

It's the moment that, after weeks or even months of working with a person, I suddenly look and say, "Oh! There you are!" And no matter how many times I experience it, that moment never fails to make me grin, shed a tear, fist pump or even do a little dance.

The power within us has become something of a cliché in recent years, with a lot of books, workshops and bloody expensive coaching packages on the market which claim to help reconnect you with your power. And they're not all wrong. But here's what I've found from my own journey of re-empowerment, not to mention from watching so many clients step back into their own places of power and wholeness too: that this isn't some one-size fits all process. If only it were that easy.

We have been disconnected from our power in so many ways and by so many things. Some of those are the generic impacts of a world that has removed Her from so much of the His-story we have been taught, erased whole cultures, painted power as something we have to earn or be granted and gone to great lengths to remind us of all the ways we are "too much" or "not enough." These are all things we can be reminded of and supported through, in order to help us work through the bullshit and remember the full scope of possibility.

But so many of those books and courses will only go so far, failing to take into account the many personal wounds, shadows and blockages that are stopping us recognising what power truly looks like for us, never mind returning to that place of power for ourselves.

Doing that might well take in more books and courses – it definitely did for me. But more of it – actually much, much more of it – was about me taking time to sit with myself and gaining support to reconnect with what it truly meant to understand what power looked and felt like for me. Recognising where and when I personally felt most powerful; and overcoming the fears that were holding me back from stepping into those feelings of my own power more regularly.

I won't tell you that process means I feel completely in my power and totally awesome in every moment of every day. Let's not forget the ebb and flow of our lives in every way, including power. There are times our connection to this inner power of ours will waver, but that's not because our power wavers, only because our belief in that power does. And the more we work on the stuff behind the scenes, sitting in that place of fear and listening to what it has to say before choosing to follow the path that feels most grounded and powerful in that moment, the shorter those periods of disempowerment become.

The path out of those moments of wavering so often comes when we choose to do something that makes us feel most like ourselves and surrender to the knowledge that that is the most powerful we can ever be.

When it comes to the use of this inner power, it feels important to talk about witchcraft. Personally, I always wanted to be a witch. As a kid my favourite book was *The Worst Witch* (it's a sign of my age that Hermione Grainger didn't arrive in my life until my late teens). As a teenager *The Craft* was my favourite movie and even today I will happily watch anything with witches in. But even after years of buying incense, using tarot cards and working with spirit, it took a long time for me to call myself a witch. Because witches were powerful, and I felt anything but.

Before I claimed that label for myself, I spent years leading a working coven and teaching a group of women about what it was to be a witch, and even longer learning about the history of witchcraft and doing what I could to align myself with the energies I spoke about.

Recently, one of the most powerful women I know spoke to me about the idea of witchcraft. She told me that she felt the same way about spells as she had about praying as a teenager; as though she was begging or pleading for help in a way that was not at all powerful.

In many ways I understood, because in those early days of tiptoeing around my power that's exactly what I felt I was doing.

I'm not sure what changed along the way. Maybe it was that dialogue with my power, or maybe it was the healing, remembrance and integration that followed. But at some point I came to not only remember what it was to be a witch, but also to be that witch.

The truth is that it's not – and never has been – about begging for help with anything, any more than it was about remembering every correspondence or historical fact in the books or on the websites. Instead it was about trusting my own power to make change.

Then about working with the archetypal energies reflected in my own tarot deck and the lists of deities in my books, with the power of the elements and with, well, the everything – the light and the dark, the Sun and the Moon, the Earth and the Sky, the God and the Goddess and all that lies above, below and in between – connecting with those, respecting them and balancing them all in order to make those things happen.

It turns out that oh-so-clichéd line from the Wizard of Oz is actually a pretty important one when it comes to truly embracing the identity of a witch: "You've always had the power my dear. You just had to remember for yourself."

That power is one you tap into every time you put your feet on the Earth and recognise yourself as a child of this planet, and every time you stare up at the stars and take your place as a citizen of this Universe.

It's a power we acknowledge when we make a wish on a candle, just as much as when we make a conscious decision to walk away from something that is no longer serving us.

It's a force that is as evident in our connection to a crystal or a cauldron as to a leaf or a cherished t-shirt.

And while witchcraft, like any other belief system, is a sacred practice that should be approached with respect, with a number of fundamental principles that should be learned and put into practice appropriately in order to both respect those traditions and keep ourselves safe – circle casting, protection and the need to harm none for starters; it is also in many-ways the anti-religion.

Instead of being told where we worship, we find the places that feel sacred for ourselves.

Instead of being told who we worship and pointed in the direction of a disconnected deity who needs conduits to pass messages on for us, we find the deities that resonate with us and worship the entire world and Universe around us too, recognising as we do the power and sacredness within us as part of that Universe, and the direct contact we get to call our own and enjoy for ourselves.

And as for the rules… Well, they're certainly not on stone tablets and really are down to the witch themselves, except for a few fundamentals of the Wiccan Rede that say things like:

> *"Bide the Wiccan Laws we must, in Perfect Love and Perfect Trust. Live you must and let to live. Fairly take and fairly give…"*

> *"When ye have and hold a need, hearken not to others' greed. With a fool no season spend, lest ye be counted as his friend."*

> *"Merry meet and merry part, bright the cheeks and warm the heart.*

Mind the Threefold Law you should, three times bad and three times good.

Eight words the Wiccan Rede fulfil: an' ye harm none, do what ye will."

I'm not saying everyone has to be a witch, or even that they should. We all get to decide what is and isn't sacred for us and it is that sacredness that helps bring us home to ourselves. But for myself, claiming that label and learning to own it is one of the most empowering things I have ever done, and my practice as a witch has reconnected me to parts of myself I hadn't even realised I was missing.

I'm yet to learn how to float feathers like Bonnie Bennett from *The Vampire Diaries* or to "Alohomora" a door open à la Hermione Grainger, but it turns out it was never those things that make you a witch.

Being a witch is about respecting yourself, your power and the whole of the world around you, and carrying that respectful intention into not only your witchcraft but every breath of your day.

It's about connecting with the world for everything it is.

It's about facing up to the scariness and the darkness within and around you.

It's about doing whatever you need in order to rebalance your life and the energies around you in order to make change.

And possibly most of all, it's about believing in your own power to do exactly that.

Integration

When I think about the journey back to a place of power, I often come back to the concept of integration; a process I believe we move through every time we reclaim and reconnect with a "new" aspect of power within ourselves. Because it is within that integration that I believe we not only reconnect with our power, but also work through the fears that have kept that power hidden from us. And then we learn how to use it in a way that doesn't simply throw it out in laser eye beams at everyone who has ever wronged us.

This path of integration will often include a lot of the shadow work we mentioned earlier because for so many of us, power has become a shadow that we try to keep hidden.

Years ago, I took part in an incredible programme through which I was invited – loudly and proudly – to call back my power regularly.

Doing that always felt potent, as though I was putting out a call to a part of myself I had long since disconnected from. But never in all those times of calling, was I able to fully connect with the wholeness of the force I felt waiting in the wings.

One day in meditation about a year after the programme ended, I decided it was time to call upon that power of mine again and dialogue with it a little, asking what else I had to do in order to fully integrate her into my life. The conversation went a little like this:

"I call back my power from all times and all places."

Whisper from somewhere in the depths of my subconscious: *"Hello?"*

"Hi! Welcome! It's so good to talk to you again. But I feel like we've been talking for a while now, so I wondered what's stopping us from taking the next step and re-connecting properly, fully?"

Deep breath. *"Honestly? I'm not sure you really want to. I'm not sure I really want to!"*

"Whaaaat? Gods no, I totally want to be powerful. I'm all for it. I have those priestess memories right? And they were awesome!"

"They were, it's true. But you remember how that ended right?"

She wasn't wrong. After all, in my work with past lives I had seen a lot of powerful life experiences; all of which had ended badly. Not least a lifetime as a priestess in ancient Babylon which ended with the pillaging of my whole community, the murder of my whole family and my own kidnap, torture and eventual death. Even now the thought of how that lifetime ended is painful, is it any wonder I was more than a little scared of fully embracing my power?

"OK, yes. I get that. But that was literally hundreds of years ago, I know things aren't the same now."

"True. But you also know it's still unsafe in a different way to be empowered, right?"

"Oh. Yes." I guess she was talking about the ex who did everything in his power to tell me my beliefs were ridiculous. About the former work colleague who shouted in my face when I tried to disagree with their way of doing things. Or maybe about the times I had been told I was too feminine to get a promotion at work. Then there were those times that flirting or even just being kind to men had been called out as a sign that I was a "slut" who should keep away from men, shutting down a part of me that had always felt so naturally powerful.

"OK yes, you're right. But we're more powerful than all of those things, right?"

"*Definitely. 100%. But you know that there is a lot to work through there, and that you really need to believe in this – in us.*"

Deep breath. "OK. I can do that. It might be hard, but I can do it. How do I prove that to you?"

"*Start by welcoming me back. You call me, but then you keep me at arm's length. It doesn't exactly make me want to stay.*"

And so began a process of re-integration that meant letting go of so many of those past experiences as being exactly that – experiences that lived in the past and had no right to define who I am now or how powerful I can be in future. Meanwhile I was diving into other memories too, until I understood what it was about them that had made me so determined to hide from my power for so long.

It was a process that involved me listening to people I respected as they complimented me, and sitting in the discomfort of those compliments until they had integrated with what I already knew and suspected about myself, in order to understand how I could use those things for my own benefit.

And possibly most of all, it was a process of fortification in myself and my power which told me that no matter what the outside world said to me; no matter how many times I was called out for being "not enough" of something or "too much" of something else, I could stay connected to that power, rooted into my needs and to a knowing of what it truly means to be me.

The Sixth Key: RESPONSIBILITY

As a geek talking about power, of course I am going to quote Spiderman's Uncle Ben when I remind you that with great power comes great responsibility. But to include that as the key to this chapter will likely come as no surprise to you.

After all, when we look at the power structures of the world today one thing we see time and time again, is a reluctance to take true responsibility for the problems that occur. Consider the politicians who are all too keen to talk about their successes but will hastily change the subject of an interview any time their less successful policies are called into question; and consider the way the worst managers in any job are inevitably those who will pass the buck onto someone beneath them any time something bad happens. Now think instead about the flipside of that; those leaders that are unafraid to take full responsibility when something goes wrong before offering a safe space in which the people they work with can come together to find a solution and a new way of doing things.

When it comes to using your own power, it is – unsurprisingly – the second group of leaders that you want to follow in the footsteps of, remembering that your power and how you use it is your own responsibility. The Wiccan Rede is pretty clear on the idea of the "law of three" – that what you put out into the world comes back to you threefold, and whether you call it karma, the law of attraction or just simple justice, that is something I've definitely witnessed in the past and experienced for myself too; a cautionary tale any time you are tempted to use your own power in pursuit of harm rather than help.

Admittedly, responsibility is something I have a few problems with – not because I shy away from it though, actually completely the opposite. As the oldest child of two oldest children, I have spent a lot of my life believing I should take responsibility for not only my own actions and wellbeing but also that of the people around me. Speaking from experience, I can tell you that is exhausting, but it's also the kind of mindset that can keep us from fully integrating our power, terrified that we will never be able to handle the burden of responsibility that comes when we step into a place of power.

So let me be clear: when I speak about the responsibility that comes with your power, I am referring to the responsibility for yourself and the use of your personal power, as well as for anyone or anything you have chosen to take responsibility for (a baby or a work remit for example). I am not suggesting that as you use the power of your voice to drive change in society, you are responsible for the whole of that society, or that using your power means you need to have all of the answers. In fact, there is an important aspect of humbleness that comes with the use of power. It reminds us not only of the extent of our power, but also of its limits and the fact that, no matter how well intentioned it may be, the moment we consider ourselves more powerful than someone else is undoubtedly the time we step out of that place of power within and back into the dynamic of power over which we have all seen go so wrong.

EXERCISES AND PROMPTS

MEDITATIONS

Reconnecting with your power: Let's get to know our own power. What does yours look and feel like? In this journey we will reconnect with that power so that you can begin to recognise and work more closely with it.

Plugging back into your main power sources: All power comes from an original source, and in this meditative journey – which can be repeated as often as feels right – we will plug your own connection back in to the Heart of Gaia, Divine Source and the Cosmic centre of potential.

RITUAL

Opening the door to your power: The journey back to embrace our power completely is different for all of us, but each journey starts with the choice to open a door back to that power. This ritual will support you to do exactly that, and give the first steps of guidance on what to do with any insights you receive there.

EXERCISES

- Put on the song that makes you feel most powerful and dance your ass off. Mine throughout the entire writing of this book has been You Should See Me in A Crown by Billie Eilish.

- Where do you feel most powerful? Consider what it is about those places, situations and activities which brings you that sense of power and see where you can lean into those feelings and experiences more in other areas of your life.

- Think about the places in which you can use your power to make change. The secret answer for this is everywhere. Even if the change you make is as simple as swapping out what you eat for lunch or writing in a different coloured ink, see what changes can be inspired by taking back your power over a small change.

JOURNAL PROMPTS

- What does power mean to you?

- What are your unique powers and abilities? What would the people closest to you call your superpowers?

- What would it mean to you to be powerful?

- When you think about being powerful does that feel at all scary? If so why, what does this bring up for you?

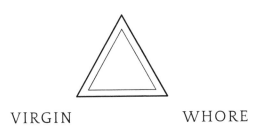

EMPOWERMENT

VIRGIN   WHORE

Before I go any further, let me issue a trigger warning for rape and sexual violence. If that's something you have experienced and don't want to write about, then please treat yourself especially tenderly as you move through this chapter. I won't tell you to avoid the chapter entirely because I believe that a reclamation of our sexual power is something that is available to and important for all of us. But I do invite you to go gently, and to seek support in moving through the coming pages, as and where you need it.

Sex is one of the biggest taboos of our time, particularly for anyone who is not a gregarious and attractive white, cisgender, heterosexual man. Anyone who fits into that stereotype has, for the longest time, been able to do whatever they please sexually with whomever they please – as many whomevers as they please, in fact – with no more than an eye roll and a "boys will be boys" joke, while anyone outside of that stereotype is likely to receive a very different reaction.

For women, sex is a particularly taboo subject – one in which we are encouraged to show as little interest as possible to avoid being called out as the promiscuous "whore," unless it is inside the bedroom with a committed partner – when we are equally criticised for both anything out of the "ordinary" that we choose to do and anything we refuse to do.

It's not hard to see where this has come from. And I don't mean the culture that paints girls as sex objects from the second they begin to look like teenagers, if not before. Although that is definitely a huge factor in itself. But above and beyond that, this comes down to fear.

There are many ways that the wisdom and power once considered to have belonged to women has been taken over the years. It has either been adopted by patriarchy through the lens of professionalism or education, or cast aside and diminished as worthless. But – no matter how much they may have tried to interfere with the process – there is one thing the patriarchy is yet to figure out how to do without a womb: gestate and birth life.

I know, we likely aren't too far from being able to clone people in labs or create androids with artificial intelligence, but traditionally there is only one way to bring new human life into the world, and that wasn't something the patriarchy was capable of alone. That in itself – together with the practically superhuman feats of strength and endurance a person goes through during pregnancy and childbirth – is powerful to the point of terrifying for anyone in pursuit of ultimate power over others.

With that in mind is it any wonder that the conduit to that power – sex – has been banished and controlled, allowable only on the terms of those who wish to continue the species they want to dominate?

Bleurgh, even writing that makes me feel sick.

But that is really the foundation for this chapter, and for the duality that puts women as either virgin – the innocent and pure caregiver whose only physical dalliances are to bring children into the world. Or whore – she who ignores all societal conditioning and takes sexuality into our own hands on her own terms.

The virgin

Once upon a time the word "virgin" meant a woman who was wholly her own; one that was unmarried and undoubtedly mistress of her own destiny. But in the years since, as we know all too well, it has come to mean something very different – someone who has never experienced physical sex and is, consequently, seen as "pure."

For those who identify as men, the word virgin is an insult – a word thrown in the direction of anyone not considered to be sexually confident or promiscuous. While for those who identify as women, it is the status Western society asks of all of us, criticising anyone who steps off that path of sexual innocence, while at the very same time refusing to allow us to occupy that position in a world that sexualises us almost as soon as we identify ourselves as girl in the world.

So many of us have no conscious experience of what it is not to be sexualised; not to be criticised for the perceived sexuality or androgyny of our clothes; not to be expected to put our own physical attractiveness at the forefront of our consideration as soon as we put ourselves out into the world; not to mind our behaviour in case it is deemed too flirty or sexual and "inviting" of unwanted attention; and not to be asked, from the moment we are old enough to be considered adults, when we plan to have children.

That type of conditioning is an abuse in its own right; gaslighting us to consider ourselves through the lens of sexuality and providing an intrinsic veil of shame through which we see ourselves, even before we form our own self opinion.

Despite their emphasis upon it, the true title of virgin is one that the patriarchy does everything in its power to restrict from women. Today, the word has been twisted to mean subservient; someone who is willing to do exactly as they are told when it comes to sex – fertile and happy to step into that power of creation only when the time comes to create life. Otherwise? Otherwise that part of themselves should be tucked away and forgotten about to ensure it can't be used for anything that might upset the balance of things.

As an aside here, it is no surprise that until very recently, those women who are no longer fertile, tended to either disappear from our media altogether or be cast as villains and hags in our stories; terrifying creatures we should all be wary of, rather than looking up to for the wild wisdom they have gathered on their journey through and out of virginhood. Wisdom they will likely be willing to share freely and passionately with the world around them, if only we give them a platform or let them close enough to be heard.

In a way, the personification of the virgin as good and sexually submissive, ties in with suppression of the ancient Hieros Gamos. This was a once-sacred ritual in which sexually confident and powerful priestesses stood in for the sovereignty Goddess of the land. Would-be leaders had to work hard to earn her approval before they would be allowed anywhere near her bed or a position of stewardship over that land. Maybe this is why so many of the Goddesses we associate with sovereignty over the land are also seen through the lens of the nurturing, benevolent healers and Mothers, and represent those positive, light-filled representations of the Divine Feminine that we are encouraged to work with when we first begin our tiptoed journey back towards that energy.

Consider the story of Guinevere in the Arthurian legends of my own lands; a woman who is always cast as the beautiful and usually virtuous romantic heroine who marries the King and serves happily beside him (until we reach the point in the story when she cheats on her husband with his best friend Sir Lancelot, but that's a story for another day!) in comparison to Morgan Le Fae, the Sorceress sister of Arthur who owns her power and is often cast as the villain responsible for his eventual downfall. Even our mythology has sold us a version of the "light" and the "dark" goddesses; those to be worshipped as good and those unafraid to own their power who should consequently be feared as evil.

But even as I prepare to launch a defence of the dark and terrifyingly powerful Goddess who owns her sexuality, I should say that there is nothing wrong with a woman who chooses to claim the mantle of virgin as her own in any way. A person's sexuality is theirs to do with whatever they choose; be that to share with others or to keep for themselves; to utilise as a means of creating life or to lean into simply because it feels bloody good. Sex can be as powerful and beautiful gift to keep to oneself as it can be to share, with no one choice better or worse than another. But the key word there is choice.

The virgin archetype is powerful as long as it is used in the traditional way, to represent someone who chooses to make their sexuality wholly their own. Unfortunately for many of us, much like the priestesses in the later, twisted versions of the Hieros Gamos, that choice was taken away from us when our sexuality became something the patriarchy claimed as its own.

It's hard to write about sex without talking about the word shame. After all, in today's world, the two so often go hand in hand for so many of us; particularly for members of the LGBTQIA+ community, whose sexuality is dismissed and shamed by our heteronormative culture; and for those who are Disabled, older or fat and therefore deemed unworthy of sexuality in general.

The only time sex can be spoken about without whispers is generally when a heterosexual couple – ideally young and married – are trying to conceive a child. Otherwise we whisper, use euphemisms or avoid the subject entirely. Hell, even as I write this I feel uncomfortable that I'm talking about sex and hope my grandma might skip this chapter (hi Grandma!). But that shame causes problems.

First of all, because shame is such a heavy energy. According to psychiatrist David R Hawkins, shame is the lowest level of consciousness we humans can carry, something that drains us and drags us down further than any other feeling we can embody, bringing all manner of physical, emotional and energetic problems as a result.

And when it comes to sex, how much damage does that shame cause? How many of us struggle with sexual trauma or discomfort because we're ashamed to talk to anyone about the things that trouble us? From the simple "I don't know how to..." to the complex, "I can't bear to be in my own head because of what I've experienced," so many of our experiences go unheard and unhealed because of the shame that is practically bred into us around sex.

I have lost track of the number of clients over the years who have unearthed a huge experience of sexual trauma midway through our work together. Yup, midway through. Because despite the significant impact that experience may have had on them, their lives and relationships, they've spent years downplaying it and claiming it wasn't important with lines like:

"It can't be rape because we were in a relationship."

"I can't claim that as a trauma because I was drunk."

"It was consensual until the last minute. How can I complain about it if I kissed him?"

"Yes it was sexual assault, but it wasn't violent so I was lucky really."

And the one I've heard most of all?

"No, it wasn't consensual. But I can't really say I was raped."

I get it. The word "rape" is in itself so triggering that it's often easier to use phrases like "non-consensual" and "I didn't really want to," than to acknowledge what happened to us.

But when we acknowledge the negative sexual experiences that weren't our fault. And let me be clear, whatever this world has told us, any sexual experience that you did not or could not consent to was neither your choice nor your fault. Then we can begin to let go of the shame that has prevented us from dealing with that trauma. And as that happens, we enable ourselves to heal.

We take back our bodies, our minds, our safety, our choice and our power from whichever bastard(s) tried to claim it – and us – as theirs.

Not only from our own bad, painful or traumatic experiences, but from generations and lifetimes of being disconnected from our sexual power. It will come as no surprise to you that the Hieros Gamos I described earlier became, over time, far less than sacred, as would-be rulers stopped considering the consent of a priestess as a key ingredient in that ritual and, rather than being granted sovereignty over the land and her body, they took it at whatever cost that required.

It's no coincidence that the de-sanctification of that ritual was followed by the continual rape of our planet for her resources; or that at around the time rulers stopped engaging in this act of sovereignty, invading forces also stopped even pretending to respect the lives and ways of those whose lands they stole, and colonisation and oppression became the norm.

The journey to recover sovereignty over our own sexuality can be – as we know all too well – a long and arduous one that begins with the empowerment of those who have been oppressed. But I wonder if that journey also has to involve the re-empowerment of *what* was once considered sacred too.

We recognise ourselves as those true virgins who are and have always been our own, and then move forward with our lives in exactly the way those patriarchal forces have been so terrified of us doing, from a place of power.

Reclaiming our sexual freedom

You may be wondering why I included the topic of shame and sexual assault within the "virgin" section of this chapter. The answer is simple, because I want to remind us all that non-consensual sex is never a choice that we make. **Never.**

The dominating forces in our out of balance world will tell us otherwise. As we all know only too well, they will tell us that any woman who chooses to be sexually confident "deserves" pain and assault. That revealing clothes, letting down our inhibitions, confidently having sex for fun or any manner of other behaviours they have labelled as sinful mean that we are inviting sexual attention from whoever wants to give it to us, and that we should take responsibility for whatever happens following that.

That is bullshit.

In fact, the very idea that any consensual sexual behaviour should be considered sinful; not to mention the idea that anyone can and should pass judgment on our sexual choices at all, is bullshit, and if those are statements I need to repeat daily or hourly until every person in our societies remembers them then you can be damned sure I will do that.

Why? Because no matter how many clients I support through the journey of reclaiming that power and joy from those who would have taken it for them, the very fact we are still having those conversations never fails to light a fire of sacred rage in my belly that tells me this must change.

And because I am sick and tired of seeing incredible people shamed away from something that is not only a joy of human life but also a power; a power that we have been disconnected from for far too long.

We have all witnessed or heard stories of someone who is in a place of seduction; a place in which another person has entranced them so completely that they will willingly do anything just to stay there. Hell, some of us have maybe even been in that place ourselves. Because in many ways it is a completely natural state of being. Harnessing the power of creation within us and owning who we are – every bit of ourselves in our full, naked glory. And getting intimate with that until we can stand tall, firm, whole and powerful in ourselves, as we enjoy and immerse ourselves in the pleasure such confidence offers – the kind of bone-tremoring, face-contorting, soul cleansing, uncontrollable, need a few minutes to recover, pleasure that can only come when we have stepped out of a place of fear and into a point of our own wholeness.

Then taking that power out into the world – whether directing it towards another person or not – in a way that they cannot help to be magnetised by. Not because of how damned hot we are (although it's a knocking bet that we are indeed hot stuff) but because of the fact that confidence breeds confidence and they too want to enjoy the kind of power and pleasure that we are so clearly enjoying for ourselves.

When we come from a place of our own wholeness, that seduction is a wonder to behold and to be a part of. It is arguably one of the single most awesome experiences we can have as a human and – when it reaches the point of connection physically or otherwise – one of the most sacred activities we can be involved in.

But for those who struggle to put themselves in a place of such wholeness, seductive energy isn't something to be respected or honoured, but something to be resented or even feared.

I spent a number of years working in a hideously sexist environment; one in which men were not only allowed but almost expected to do exactly as they pleased, with all displays of sexuality or aggression considered an example of how "boys will be boys" while women were held to very different standards. I and other women there were slut shamed for anything from wearing skirts or talking to a man, while also being unashamedly harassed by some of those men, regardless of what we did or didn't do to avoid their stereotypes. For a long time, I carried my experiences there – both the choices I had made and those that had been taken away from me – as shameful proof that I was somehow "less than" the woman and the feminist that I wanted to be. But in recent years I have realised something more important:

That all of the gossiping, criticism, bullying and dismissing was because the ringleaders of that gang were terrified of women in their power; terrified that maybe someone less physically dominant than them could turn out to have a greater sense of power and control than they could ever have dreamed of – not only upsetting their own positions at the top of the tree, but also making no secret of the fact that the physical prowess and positions of leadership they claimed to be most influential, were actually nothing of the sort.

Of course, whether the individuals behind that culture consciously knew that was their reasoning, is another story. For so many, this toxically abusive approach to sex and sexuality has gone on for so many lifetimes and generations that they have no idea what is behind it. Like the invaders who raped priestesses of sovereignty in order to stake their claim to lands that could never have been theirs, the witch hunters of the Middle Ages who called out anyone whose wisdom and connection was respected more than the systems they themselves were trying to embed. And even today the people who vilify sex workers and deem them unworthy of safety or regulation, rather than clamping down, the people running those industries without care or respect. All they know is that those who are connected to that lunar energy of seduction are a dangerous threat to their quest for dominion and must be subdued.

Earlier I wrote about the "light" energies so many of us work with when we first reconnect with the Goddess. Yet there are a whole raft of archetypes and associated figures out there that so many of the books hailing the return of the Divine Feminine refuse to speak about unless they've been repainted as shiny, pretty and otherwise socially acceptable. Our culture tells us that the "dark" goddess – she who is not so virginal and peaceful – is in some way evil, terrifying, destructive and very much deserving of the name whore. But none of that is true.

Well OK, maybe the terrifying part is true to those who don't take the time to understand these figures, who try so desperately to keep us focussed on only the light side of our world. For those people, the goddesses who aren't just unafraid of the darkness within themselves and the world, but have journeyed there deeply enough to learn all the secrets it has to offer, must be terrifying because they challenge so many of the norms we've become accustomed to and have access to powers those people are too afraid to dream of. But that doesn't make them evil, or even needlessly destructive.

Yes, there are Goddesses like the Egyptian Sekhmet and Hindu Kali Ma who will rage into feasts and battlefields with the force of an army and destroy all that lies in their path. But their destruction is never selfish. It comes from the kind of ferocious love that makes us lash out to protect who and what matters.

And yes, there are those figures associated with death, like the Irish Morrigan and the Norse Freyja who foretell death and war, and carry fallen troops over to the Afterlife, but they don't cause that death, only hold the space for it.

When I formally began the Divine Feminist podcast a few years back, I called in a patron for the project. There was a New Moon ritual in which I invoked the energy of Divine Feminism, spelled out everything I wanted the podcast and any related work to be, and then opened the space for spirit to collaborate with me on this and for the energetic patron of it all to step forward. Enter Lilith. Yes, Lilith.

If you aren't familiar with Lilith let me give you a quick recap of her story. It is said that she was the first woman on Earth and the first wife of Adam, sculpted from the dirt at the same time he was and sent off to populate the paradisiacal garden of Eden with him. She was told it would be fine; that within that garden she would find everything she could ever need and want, but slowly Lilith began to see through the cracks.

She started to grow bored with the simple life, began to wonder if maybe the walls of the garden weren't there to protect her but instead to restrict her, and figured that maybe, just maybe, it was time she mixed things up a little. Which is probably what led her to ask Adam if the next time they had sex, maybe she could go on top instead of lying back and thinking of Eden as she had every time so far?

Adam was furious. How dare she? Didn't she know that as a woman she was subservient to him and should therefore lie beneath him?

God was furious. Didn't she know sex wasn't about pleasure and fun, but was all about making babies in the most perfunctory way possible? She would get on her back and like it thank you.

Lilith's response? She sprouted giant black wings and flew out of Eden, giving them the finger on her way (OK, I added that last bit myself, but I like it). With that Lilith was written out of the Bible, and out of the history of humanity itself unless as the Mother of demons or vampires, consort of Satan or evil demoness in her own right in all manner of movies, books and TV shows. To see her portrayed in that way has become such a cliché that I now audibly groan when she turns up as the villain in something I'm watching or reading.

However, when she turned up as the patron for this work, I admit that even I got a little bit nervous. After all this was the original wild woman, the one who had not only given patriarchy the original F-U, but had also suffered the consequences as a result. And while I was all for the former, the latter definitely scared me and made me wonder if my work too would include a journey out into the desolate darkness that lay outside of everything I knew.

But here's what Lilith has taught me – and continues to teach me even as I write this book. That her journey over those walls wasn't an ending but a liberation; a journey into the wildness which brought fear and pain for certain, but also pain which brought joy and wisdom, and the realisation of just how expansive and wonderful the world can truly be when we reclaim the power over our own bodies and experience of human life.

When done properly, in a way that is enjoyed by everyone involved, sex is a brilliant way to release tension or pent up emotions, an excellent way to get out of our heads and into our bodies, one of the most enjoyable forms of physical exercise we can have, a beautiful way to connect with someone we care about, and a truly wonderful way to connect with our own power. What sort of shitty, restrictive culture tells us that is bad?

One that is terrified of the liberation that such an experience can offer us, and of the power it can release. You'll notice that in the previous paragraph I used the phrase "when done properly", and this is an important factor to mention in this chapter. Because when we talk about the sexually liberated women that patriarchy is so keen to call a whore, it's important to remember there are two sides to this:

The first is the truly liberated woman who, much like Lilith, owns her body and her sexuality freely and on her own terms, giving not one shit what anyone else thinks except for those she is welcoming into her bed.

The second is those whose sexuality is very much a part of her life, but in a way that feels not in the slightest bit empowered. This is the woman who sleeps with multiple partners, not because she wants to, but because she is longing for the external validation that physical connection seems to bring her, even if just for a few minutes. She often uses sex to numb out a constant heartbeat of pain and shame; and lets down her physical boundaries, not because she wants and trusts another person within them, but because those boundaries have been torn down by outside forces so many times in the past that she no longer feels safe to say no.

The patriarchy and its supporters will still criticise, shame and vilify those women. Hell, if experience tells me anything it's that many of those women will still criticise and shame themselves. Without stopping to consider just how dangerous it can be to us on every level when, after years of sex being used as a weapon against them, a person turns that weapon on themselves.

As a therapist I shouldn't have favourites, but some of my favourite client experiences in the past have been with individuals who found themselves in that second category; publicly owning a label of sexually empowered while inwardly feeling anything but. It's not that I ever like seeing the pain those women were in, but I love and have always loved the moments where they came to realise that sexuality was something they could truly own for themselves on their own terms; not a facet of life that had to be defined for them by anyone else past, present or future.

Whatever your own past – or for that matter present – experiences of sex, and however you may have felt or feel about yourself as a result, let me remind you that this is possible for you too.

That sex can be a sacred and powerful part of life that you are entitled to enjoy a healthy and beautiful relationship with. And that you are so fucking worthy of reclaiming all that and more as your own.

Empowerment

It's no surprise that Lilith's journey out of a cage that had been painted as paradise began with her making a choice related to sex. Because reclaiming our sexuality is to reclaim so much more than just how good it feels to be in bed with a partner.

It is to reclaim our bodies, for the pleasure they can feel, the strength they possess and how damned sexy they are on our terms, in the face of a society that has convinced us our physical selves are somehow "wrong" unless they look and operate in a certain – at best unrealistic and at worst completely impossible way. As the incredible Sonya Renee Taylor says in her book of the same name, "Your body is not an apology," and is, by its very nature and existence, unconditionally worthy of love, care, respect and pleasure.

It is to reclaim our autonomy in a world that so often likes to define us, even today, by the sexual relationships we are part of. It is to remind the world that whoever we may or may not be sleeping with, and whatever commitments we may or may not have made to those people, just like those original virgins, we are whole in ourselves.

It is to reclaim a sense of connection to those partners we do choose to let into our lives and our bodies – not just physically, although definitely that too. Because when we choose to engage our sexuality from a place of connection and communion rather than climax and power, physical sex cannot help but improve for us. After all, as Herman Hesse writes in Siddhartha, "One cannot take pleasure without giving pleasure". Emotionally, and in terms of those non-physical connections we have with those people, our relationships cannot help but deepen and improve. Of course this is a complex subject in itself, but imagine the way an overall connection with someone is strengthened when you are comfortable to be at your most physically vulnerable with them and still set a boundary, express a need, or otherwise risk rejection? Of course there will be some partners who will be intimidated by this, but pretty quickly we start to realise those aren't the partners deserving of us.

Perhaps more than the connection with our partners though, reclaiming our sexual power is to reclaim a connection to ourselves. One that reminds us we are safe to be trusted and recognises us as the trusted stewards of our bodies, our emotions and our pleasures. It is a connection that allows us to reclaim sexual pleasure for the shameless joy and beauty that it can be – whether alone or otherwise. A connection that trusts us to not only get to know the inner and outer terrain of ourselves but to recognise and honour its beauty and worthiness at every possible turn.

And to reclaim our sexuality is to reclaim so much of our power.

Not only the power for creativity; because whether we choose to create life or not – hell, whether we even choose to engage in the kind of sexual acts that could create life – it is important to remember the creative potential that lives within our sexual organs is one of the most powerful energetic forces we have available us. After all there is a reason why sex magic is so damned powerful; why it was used so frequently in the ancient world – a world that truly respected and honoured it – and why, even today, so many books are written specifically on the subject. A world that has limited that energy, has in turn limited our access so creativity, and so many possibilities as a result.

But also the power of seduction, enchantment, connection. Consider the ways that the natural world enchants and seduces you with every sunset over the ocean or with the song of the birds and colours of the flowers on a fresh summer's morning? It is so incredibly natural and so heart-wrenchingly beautiful.

We too have access to that power; something we have been told is evil and manipulative by those who want all the power in the world for themselves. And let's be honest, it could be – any force allowed to swing out of balance or used with the wrong intention can be dangerous. But when used with positive intent; when used from a place of true connection, that power can be an incredible force that offers beauty and pleasure for everyone involved.

In some ways that power, and the sexuality it comes from, can be difficult to comprehend – difficult even to write about – because we have been so disconnected from it for so long. But true sexuality is the kind of power and potency that enables us to feel both in flow with everything around us and able to create whatever we want and need.

Sexuality isn't about just an intimate act between people or done alone, it is so much more. And it is time to reclaim the fullness of that for ourselves.

The Seventh Key: PLEASURE

Done right, sex is about two things; connection and pleasure. And since, arguably, connection is the root of pleasure then we can cut that down to one thing.

Sexual pleasure isn't just about what happens in the bedroom or with another person. It's about the kind of all-encompassing pleasure that comes from allowing ourselves to be in that powerful flow we spoke of; a pleasure that can be found anywhere and anytime we let our defences down and truly allow ourselves to connect to its essence. It's something we find at times when we're out in nature, indulging in the sensual pleasure of good food, in the rapturous place of carelessly moving our bodies to good music, even that "eureka" moment of an incredible discovery or realisation.

Being wholly in that, unashamedly full of it, and allowing ourselves to really feel it? That creates a sensuality and a sexuality that cannot be explained so well in words.

The problem so often though, is that in a world so keen to tell us that pleasure is a decadence we should feel guilty for experiencing, many of us scarcely know what is pleasurable to us. Or even what true, shameless pleasure feels like, not to mention take the time to regularly go out and embrace things that put us in touch with our own pleasure, whatever they may be.

As part of my own journey to reconnect with myself and my body after years of bad relationship choices and the toxically sexist environment I spoke of earlier, I took two years away from any sort of romantic relationship. Initially, that came from a place of fear, but very quickly it became less about not connecting to other people and more instead about choosing to re-connect to myself and that sense of pleasure on my terms.

Of course, you don't need to go to quite that extreme. But I do invite you to take the time to unpack and unpick that idea of pleasure; what it truly means to you, where you have and haven't experienced it in the past and even where and how you experience it today.

There is often a lot of talk about gratitude lists – something I have personally found so much benefit from over the years. But my consciously single period led me to keep a pleasure list – an ever-growing record of the things I like and enjoy, and those that feel good in all of their different forms.

This subject of pleasure is definitely one to dive deep on and check in on yourself with – including where physical sex is concerned – rather than to assume that what feels good is what you have always expected or been told.

And again, whatever those deep dives reveal, I want to remind you that pleasure is something you are worthy of and entitled to.

EXERCISES AND PROMPTS

MEDITATION

Meeting the Dark Goddess: Journey with me to meet the Dark Goddess in whichever form She appears to you. Remember though, She's not always as scary as the world would like you to believe!

RITUAL

Sexual release ritual: Whatever your own personal sexual past, we all carry so much pain and shame within us on this topic. This ritual, best done during the Waning Moon, will support you in releasing the sexual wounds and burdens that are carried within you to allow you to move forwards more freely.

EXERCISES

- Spend a day making choices for pleasure. Ideally make it a day when you are completely free from responsibilities and can make every single choice from a place of what feels good. See what you do, how that feels and where the day takes you.

- Put on a track that makes you feel truly sexy and dance. If you're really feeling the pull then wear an outfit in which you feel best. Hell, go all out and prepare as though you were out for a hot date with a partner and then dance like no-one's watching... Or like someone incredible is watching, and can see you for the sexy and empowered being that you are.

- Put aside a good chunk of time and spend that sensually pleasuring yourself. Maybe this is about sexual touch, but maybe it's equally about something else instead or as well; a beautifully scented candle, sensual music; whatever it takes to put you in that flow of pleasure.

JOURNAL PROMPTS

- Begin keeping your own pleasure list – maybe as something you do each day or maybe as one large list that grows over time and includes everything and anything you personally found pleasurable.

- What does sex mean to you?

- Chronicle your sexual experiences. Which were bad, why is that and what made them feel that way or left that impression upon you? Equally which were good, why is that and what happened to make that the case?

- What have you learned about sex from society, from others around you, and from the experiences you have had?

- What would you need to feel truly safe and pleasured sexually?

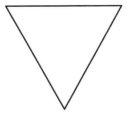

water

The elixir of life, cleanser of ways and first home any of us knew.

Water is the new beginning that formed our gateway to the world, the life force which cools, soothes and gives us all we need to go on.

It is the quenching of thirst when we're hot and tired and the crash of a wave that wakes us from a slumber of stagnation.

We welcome it in the West, with the changing colours of Autumn, the cooling of the afternoon and the calls and dance of the wild one.

In Water, we find the emotion, its ebbs and flows as they steer our heart through life.

With Water comes the gentle rains that wash away the old and coax colour and beauty to life around us.

To forget Water is to be parched and dry, unable to connect with ourselves and our hearts. It is to be without that which is within us and that which is the very source of our planet.

To restrict the Water is to kill; to deaden the humanity with life itself not far behind.

But to allow Water to pour upon us undammed, is to drown all that we are in a wave that takes the breath away; a tsunami that can destroy all we hold dear.

It is to fall into a whirlpool of feeling where the feet cannot find solid ground and nothing but nothing can stand on its own.

But Water is the moments of understanding when we see our reflection and the offer of a change when a long-awaited tide finally turns. It calls us to live in balance and asks that it may do the same.

And so we call to the West and to Water. To the setting of the Sun and the wild woman, the Autumn and the waning of the Moon.

We call to the whales and the dolphins, to the tides and the pools, to the cleansing seas, the gentle rains and the undines that swim and dance in the waves.

And we ask them to join with us, to work with us and to bless us with their cooling, their cleansing and their reflectiveness, as our journey to sacred balance continues.

To Water and the West, hail and welcome.

May it be so.

To hear this invocation in full along with a short story,
The Well That Holds All Dreams, visit the
additional materials link at the back of the book.

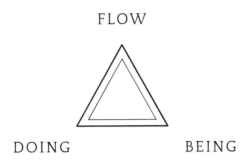

FLOW

DOING   BEING

A few years back, I was channelling some guidance for a client when the following sentence appeared on the screen in front of me:

You are a human being, not a human doing. The clue has always been in the name.

It stopped me in my tracks as possibly the most profound thing that had ever come out of my fingers. So profound, in fact, that I wish I could claim credit rather than having channelled it from Spirit!

Still though, wherever that wisdom came from, it struck a chord with me back then and continues to strike a chord now.

When we speak of those lunar energies and their darkness, of embracing the less outwardly focused phases of the Earth and of more besides, in many ways we are talking about the idea of *being* rather than doing. Something which can be so hard to do in a world that often encourages us to judge our worth by what we achieve.

And I'm not only talking there about what we achieve in a work context. Throughout the whole of our lives nowadays, we are often encouraged to judge ourselves against some sort of checklist – I often call it the "game of life" after the old boardgame which involved adding tiny plastic people to a little plastic car to create a "family" that moved around the board. Although I'm told the game is very much modernised now, in my day its purpose was encapsulated for TV in a funky (eye roll) jingle which said: "Get a job, have money maybe, get married, have a baby!"

We are so often judged by the tangible achievements we can tick off a list and by what we have done to get ourselves closer to society's perception of "success" – an ideal that may not even be right or in any way positive for us.

But how can we ever stop to ponder whether that's the case? Or indeed to give any time or effort into re-defining terms like "success" and "fulfilment" for ourselves without ever being encouraged to step away from the action and the doing; and instead think more about the *being* – about who and how we are in life and who and how we want to be?

Doing the do

In a society that measures us according to tangible achievements, there will always be more things to do and we will always be busy.

Hell, arguably that's exactly how our oppressive, out of balance systems want us to be, because as long as we're busy, we will be too tired and distracted to ask questions or make changes. As long as we're busy, we will just keep keeping on, caught in that endless cycle of doing without ever stopping to question how much that is actually benefitting us.

And the problem with trying to be in lives that have become so full of doing is that all too often, switching off and relaxing becomes another damned thing on our to do list.

Some people will laugh at that statement. Others will recognise it as a truth that hits more than a little too close to home. Those others might just be more than a little like I once was... who am I kidding, like I occasionally still am if I let myself get too into my head.

Once upon a time my Saturday to do lists looked a bit like this:

- 9.30: Grocery shopping

- 11.30: Clean house (broken down by task of course)

- 13.30: Walk Kali

- 14.30: Wash clothes

- 14.45: Go through emails, catch up on messages I had missed throughout the week

- 15.30: Put washing out

- 15.45: Complete random life admin

- 7:00: Order/cook dinner

- 7.30: Relax

Yup, I even scheduled a specific time for relaxation. Unless of course I hadn't finished my jobs by then, at which point that relaxation time would be pushed back further because who in the hell was I to concentrate on being when there was still so much to do?

Of course that was all very productive. But that's about all it was – functional and productive, with next to no opportunity for enjoying any of it, not the relaxation at the end of the day and certainly not any of the things that led up to that point.

My greatest teacher in all of this has absolutely been my dog Kali, not only because of the way she – like all dogs – is so able to simply be in the moment, whether that's sitting in the garden with the breeze in her ears, trotting through the woods with a ball in her mouth or snuggling in for cuddles on the sofa; but also because of her ability to force me to slow down and stop. No, that's not an exaggeration, she will actually force me. For starters, Kali is the most talkative dog I have ever met, making it perfectly clear what she wants and then grumbling over and over again until she gets it. But also because she has a tendency to have physical symptoms every time I am overly stressed. And after worrying about her continuous tummy problems for years, one day I realised that her stress was clearly feeding off mine, something that was absolutely fixable.

Our animals live such short lives and to this moment, the fact it took me so long to realise this, that I wasted so much of our time together in this life working and doing, instead of being and embracing that time, breaks my heart. She – and our experience throughout our first few years together – taught me a valuable lesson, but one I wish I had learned earlier, so we could have truly enjoyed every bit of that time.

What Kali has taught me is to stop. To throw as much of the to do list as possible out of the window and instead snuggle in for a cuddle whenever and wherever I can; to take regular breaks and remember that even the busiest days can benefit from a trip to the beach or a walk in the woods.

Kali reminds me time and time again of the beauty of being, of embracing life fully for everything it is and can be. Because although I am not a believer in this being our only shot at life, I am a believer in this being our only shot at *this* life. Isn't that good enough reason to wholly embrace every single second of it and enjoy the fullness of all it can be?

But as with so much of this book, none of this is to say that we should not act. Not only do so many parts of our daily lives require our action, but our world right now stands on a precipice at which action is needed. Our action and our voices are possibly the only things which will help us to break down the imbalances, challenge the inequities and fix the sense of disempowerment that has, for so long, led us to stay in our own positions of perceived safety and privilege while this white supremacist, heteronormative, capitalistic, patriarchal, ableist society has been allowed to thrive unchecked.

This chapter is no more your permission slip to not take action on the causes that call to your heart or need your voice, than it is to not do your job, feed your children or walk your own incredible four-legged teacher.

And that doesn't only count for the big things but for the small ones in our lives too. If we want to build, to create, to move forwards, we must take action. For all of the wisdom in that "human being" philosophy, I am a firm believer we shouldn't go all the way over to that side of the scale.

If truth be told, I have had a couple of friends over the years who rebalanced themselves completely into the place of being without any of the follow through that involved doing. It was beautiful to be around for short periods of time, but those people were difficult to build long-term relationships with. It was difficult to trust them when they didn't take action on anything, and difficult to rely upon them when the very idea of doing something could often be too much for them. It's important to note that I'm not blaming or criticising either of those people for their choices, particularly since inaction can be a trauma response that leaves us stuck in freeze mode. But as with everything, we can reconnect to ourselves in order to heal any stuckness and help us to move forwards into a place of flow.

From there we can take the action ourselves or we can delegate. I will never forget a friend mocking my ex for having a house cleaner. He worked a demanding job with long hours and was often travelling on weekends, so once a month he paid a wonderful person to come in and clean his apartment. Fast forward five years until the same friend was herself in a demanding job and told me that she was now jealous – if only she had the spare cash to bring in a cleaner.

Our time is the greatest asset we have and the one we can never make more of. So doesn't it stand to reason that we would delegate the things we aren't so good at or don't enjoy so much, wherever and whenever we can?

And where that delegation isn't possible, we can still make space for being, simply by stepping back from that overwhelming sense of doing that is bred into so many of us and remembering that some things don't need to be done urgently, and others that have been drummed into us don't actually need to be done at all.

Ironically, after the story about my ex and his cleaner, I have a strong dislike for anyone who tells us our houses must always be clean. Do I like a clean, tidy house? Yes of course. And I do what I can to keep my own house as clean and tidy as possible, but does it look like a pristine show home at all times? No, because it's lived in. And because sometimes – often – what's more important than deep cleaning the hallway is sleeping, or playing in the garden, or any number of the other things that remind me how wonderful life can be.

Of course there are some jobs that must be done, and some deadlines that really are urgent. But there is always an opportunity to step back from our overwhelmingly long must-do lists and instead look for the spaces in which we can be.

We do that by looking for our why. What is it that matters? What is it that makes this task an act of service, to yourself, to those you love or to something bigger than the individual? And why is this important?

Then we allow ourselves to *be* as we *do*. We focus on carrying out each task consciously, allowing ourselves to focus wholly on whatever it is that we're doing and let ourselves feel into that physically, emotionally, mentally.

I mentioned earlier my frustration at being told my home must be pristine, but that's not to say I don't like cleaning. Every so often I love to stick on an audiobook and deep clean my entire house. I allow my mind to focus on the book while my hands are busy with the basic tasks before me, all while relishing the idea of caring for my space and reminding myself that I am worthy of a clean and beautiful home, and of providing myself with the time and energy to gift that to myself.

But there has to be a balance. We must recognise that continual doing is an addiction; an unhealthy addiction that can raise our stress levels and all of the problems that come with that, but nonetheless an addiction that serves a purpose for us. And when we try to stop it, we will go through that process of withdrawal.

I am a recovering workaholic. I spent years judging my worth by what I did. When I stopped or even tried to slow down I found it nigh on impossible. I felt worthless, beat myself up for not doing enough and realised I could only go for about ten minutes without immediately multitasking – picking up my phone, engaging in four WhatsApp conversations I'd intended to respond to earlier, googling the name of the actress I was watching and then spending 20 minutes in an IMDB wormhole, etc, etc.

Relaxation took practice. Allowing myself to relax into a state of being in which my mind wasn't whirling, took even more. It also took some hobbies that had no real purpose except for joy and bringing me into the now. Things like cross-stitching, where my hands and conscious mind had to concentrate, while the rest of me was able to relax; or ukulele playing, which takes so much focus for me that I cannot possibly do anything else at the same time.

The secret is that we are constantly human beings, even when we are doing. We just have to get ourselves back into that space as often as we can and quieten the noise of the outside world along the way.

Relaxing into being

It's fine to encourage ourselves to "simply be," but in a world that is so focussed on doing, that can be anything but simple. At best we can feel bored without a constant sense of purpose and stimulation from the world around us, and at worst we can feel guilty, worthless and all manner of other less than pleasant things.

Speaking very personally, I know that the anxiety I felt when I first tried to change my relationship with doing – an anxiety that still rears its head now from time to time – has a lot to do with the intrinsic belief that I must do more, more, more in order to live a worthy life; that I must keep going, doing and being productive even if every part of me feels overwhelmed.

For years I had a problematic relationship with alcohol, based in no small part to the fact that drinking was one of the few ways I could escape the voice telling me I should be doing *something* at all times. After all, drink enough and you will find it impossible to do... well much of anything really. And the next day? For me that was (at least) 24 hours of being physically unable to do anything but lie on the sofa eating junk food and occasionally napping. In many ways, drinking was my way of rebelling against the culture of doing at a time when, after years of being groomed for productivity, I didn't know a safe or healthy way to do that. This book will be published just over a month before my four year sober-versary, a period that has made me more familiar than ever with those "must keep doing" voices that could once be drowned out in a bottle of wine.

In the sharp silence of those early sober Saturday nights, the voices in my head felt particularly loud; the shadows we spoke about before, taking their opportunity to pop out and say hello in a mind that felt raw and overly anxious. At first that was painful – unbearable enough that I did anything and everything I could to find different ways to drown it out. Until I realised that wasn't helping, only making me more exhausted than ever, which is when mindfulness began to help.

The very idea of mindfulness has become something of a cliché nowadays, as things so often are when people share their stories without an explanation of how integrating a particular practice helped them. Personally, I don't claim to be an expert on mindfulness, but I have practiced it enough to recognise the benefits of being in the moment and transcending the many things our minds will so determinedly try to force us to focus on, rather than simply experiencing the joy of what it is to be alive.

Although for me that word "mindfulness" is also just a tad misleading. Because when we truly allow ourselves to be in any given moment, it's not only our minds that are fully present, but every part of us.

To truly be is to immerse ourselves wholly in the experience of the present moment physically, emotionally, mentally and soulfully; to step away from the voices that tell us what we should do, or what might happen if we don't and instead allow ourselves to fully and wholly be.

Yes, mindful meditation is about temporarily stepping outside of everything and allowing ourselves to get quiet. Something that is so vital in a world so full of noise. In many ways, doing that can feel like stepping outside the experience of life. But in reality it is nothing of the sort. That's why some of my most powerful experiences of mindfulness have come, not on the meditation mat, but while I've been doing something else totally consciously, fully in the moment of walking in the woods, painting the shed or cleaning.

I hear so many people say that they struggle with meditation, that their minds are too busy to get quiet and sit in silence. It's worth noting first of all that mindfulness meditations aren't about switching off your brain, but about sitting with all of the noise until you get quiet despite rather than instead of it.

In a way, that's where this leads back to the challenge of being in a world so desperate to make us *do*. When it comes instead to *being*, no-one is asking us to ignore our to do list or to force our way through that list before taking the time to be – as I learned after years of those busy Saturdays. Instead, being means recognising everything we have to do, allowing ourselves to feel through the noise of that, and then taking the time, through it all, to step back and simply allow ourselves to be.

It's easy to think that to be is simply to allow ourselves to rest, and that's certainly a part of this. Especially when we make the decision to step away from the always-on culture of doing and incorporate more being in our lives. There will inevitably be a period where we have no choice but to rest, realising just how exhausting life has previously been. And a perk of balancing out our times of action and inaction means providing ourselves with more downtime to sleep, chill out, read, watch movies or whatever else it is that gives our minds and bodies the complete and utter break they so often need, in order to stay happy and healthy. I can't recommend enough, the work of the fantastic Nap Ministry, who focus on the idea of rest as not only an act of selfcare, but also an act of rebellion – particularly for women, Black people and other oppressed groups.

But to put ourselves into the state of being, isn't just about stopping entirely. It is also about opening up space for new things to come in. A few years back (just before my time of conscious singledom), a friend asked if she could set me up for a date with another friend of hers. She spoke highly of him and he sounded nice enough, but when I looked at my diary, I realised I didn't have a spare night for over a month. A month! I vividly remember that as a moment that I realised life had to change – not necessarily because of this guy in particular, although I'm sure he was lovely. But how I could ever expect anything new and wonderful to unexpectedly appear in front of me if every moment of my life was so completely planned out?

And that doesn't just go for the physical time we have available, but for energy too. So many of us talk excitedly about the new opportunities, ideas and chapters we want to welcome into our lives, but are so damned busy that our minds, bodies and energy fields can barely keep up with what we're doing in the here and now, never mind with being able to conceive or birth something new alongside it.

To step off the hamster wheel of *doing* and give ourselves a break is to open up space and free up energy to process where we've been in the past; to process where we are right now; and then to ready ourselves for whatever is to come next. It frees up space for exactly that to happen when the time is right. Which, for the record, is often when we expect it least.

Flowing with flow

So much of this balance between doing and being is about learning to enter a true state of flow or, more specifically, a state of ebb and flow.

That means knowing that sometimes we will have more on our plates than we had hoped for, or even feel comfortable with. It means being able to recognise which of those times require us to step back and prioritise or delegate, and which require us to get our heads down and crack through more of the doing than we would usually be happy with.

And it also means recognising that there will be times which feel much more ebb-like where our diaries will be empty. Often I find that comes at exactly the time I need it most; at the end of a big project when my brain desperately needs a break or at a time when something new and unexpected arrives on the horizon and captures my attentions in a way it just couldn't have done if I had been busy.

Coming into that state of ebb and flow means surrendering to the certainty that there are times we have the answers, and other times we seem to have nothing of the sort; and recognising that is absolutely OK. We don't need to know it all and we don't always need to be in control.

That might just sound terrifying to you. I often wonder if much of the drive towards action is down to our human urge to always be in control and the misguided illusion that if only we can control every moment of our time, then nothing bad can and will ever happen.

Of course we know that's not true. We've all heard of the people who have been midway through a perfectly normal day only to get into a terrible accident, receive a life-changing call or even suddenly pass away. Bad things happen, no matter how much we busy ourselves to avoid them. But by leaning more into a state of ebb and flow, we will always be better prepared for those things when they happen.

I am generally not one for regrets, but there's one day I wish I could change. A normal Sunday when my family were together for their weekly gathering. I'd had a long day in a busy job, ahead of what I knew would be a hectic week. So I decided to stay at the office rather than head home to join them. After all, there would always be other times to have fun with them all, and this work needed to be done.

A few days later, my grandad passed away suddenly. The rest of the family had all seen him the previous weekend when they'd gathered together to laugh and talk as usual. Me though? I'd been too busy working in a job that neither fulfilled nor respected me.

No matter how much we do we can never anticipate everything that will happen. That is uncomfortable – we humans are creatures of habit and certainty after all. But it does mean we are as likely to be surprised by the good as we are the bad, and by allowing ourselves to be, we open up the space to recognise that good, the energy to allow it in and the time to enjoy it.

I often feel there is an element of magic that comes into play when we enter into this place of flow; one that offers life the opportunity to surprise us as it weaves something more wonderful than we could have expected for our next steps. Moving into a state of ebb and flow, not only opens up space for that magic to be woven, but it also offers the peace and quiet to notice and pay attention to the signs that might just guide us towards it too.

The Eighth Key: ALLOWING

When it comes to making the decision to stop doing and focus on being, so many of us are waiting for someone to tell us it's OK to pause. So the key to moving into this place of ebb and flow? Stepping out of that place of asking for permission and instead allowing yourself to do just that.

What would happen if you released the rein that gives you all of the things you must tick off a list each day? Or if you took the pressure off yourself to be busy, productive, useful and instead allowed yourself just to be whoever and whatever you need in any given moment?

As a student I worked at McDonald's, where I was regularly reminded that, "Time to lean means time to clean!" I cannot tell you how long that mantra stayed in my head whenever I took a moment to pause in my own kitchen after even the busiest of days, years later. And I also cannot tell you the liberation that came when I told that mantra exactly where it could shove its cleaning implements and instead dishes, wipe down surfaces, empty bins or generally tidy up and instead allowed myself to simply be.

I can't tell you how wonderful it felt instead, to give myself permission to dance to a song on the radio, open the back door and spend a few minutes in the garden, daydream or crouch down on the floor for a cuddle and a chat with Kali.

There are many people in the world who will take great pleasure in reminding us of all the things we should be doing during the hours that we are in their company, some of those being people you even need to listen to at times. But the moment you remember that you are ruler of your own time and energy? That is the point when you can stop with the must dos and instead allow yourself to be.

EXERCISES AND PROMPTS

MEDITATIONS

Getting mindful: This simple meditation will support you in becoming more present within your mind, body, heart and soul, and can be used whenever you need to come into the moment.

A safe space to rest: Meanwhile this journey will support you to find and create a safe and sacred space within yourself that you can return to anytime you need to rest or meditate.

RITUAL

Cutting cords of action: An opportunity to sever those energetic connections to the perpetual state of doing.

Creating a safe and sacred space to be.

EXERCISES

- Try taking a conscious walk outdoors with no distractions; no playing on your phone, listening to music or having a conversation. Allow yourself to pay attention to every aspect of your experience – indulge all of your senses and really let yourself lean into the experience of walking consciously.

- Similarly give yourself half an hour in the house to do one task. Put your phone away, turn off the TV and try not to talk to anyone, just immerse yourself in whatever it is that you're doing; how does this effect your experience?

- I invite you to try out a hobby that you do with no intention other than to keep your hands busy so that your brain can rest. Maybe this is related to craft or artwork, exercise of some sort, a musical instrument or something else entirely. Give it a go and see what happens to your mind when you let it take the backseat for a while.

JOURNAL PROMPTS

- What are your whys? Who and what is truly important to you and what is the life that you are working to create? Now, how can you allow the answers to those questions to shape your "must do" lists moving forwards?

- With that in mind, what can you let go of? What can you delegate, take your foot off the gas with or just simply stop?

- What are the ways you stop yourself from being? What are your distractions and the techniques you use to keep yourself busy even when you're not?

- Set a timer for 15 minutes and try not to do anything at all during that time. What happens? Journal on your experiences afterwards?

- Is there room in your life for surprise? Journal on what comes up for you when you think about relinquishing complete control over your schedule and opening up space.

INTERDEPENDENT

INDEPENDENT   CO-DEPENDENT

Human relationships can be one of the most challenging things in life; not only because they are forever in a state of flow, two people's energies bubbling together changing and flowing with everything that happens for each of them individually and together.

But also because of the many stories we have been told within our cultures about the ways in which those relationships should look, be and feel; how we should approach them and what they should bring to us.

Human relationships can bring so much joy and so much challenge to our lives. And the truth is, no matter how much work we do on ourselves, that may always be the case. For all the personal choices we make, we can never make decisions on how other people live their lives (and nor should we).

But it is possible to enjoy more of the joy while stepping further away from the challenge, not least by redefining the way we look at and approach those relationships.

A relationship should never involve giving up ourselves

We are so often defined by our relationships with other people. And understandably so; from the family we are raised in, to the teachers we learn from, the friends and colleagues we spend time with, romantic partners we commit to and children we raise; the people we are involved with have a big impact upon us and our lives.

Carl Jung even believed that the six people we spend the most time with, shape who we are and how we behave in the world. There is no denying our interpersonal relationships are important. But are they really as important as we are told? Important enough that we – especially those of us who identify as women – should lose ourselves in them?

I think often about the women I've known who have bounced from romantic relationship to romantic relationship with barely a pause in between to remember who they are without an "and" after or before their names. These were wonderful women who had so much to offer the world, but having been told since they were old enough to read a story that happy ever after didn't begin until they met the love of their lives, they have found it almost impossible to believe that life could ever be anything of note without a romantic partner in it.

I remember others who have stuck by difficult, unsupportive or downright abusive family members because they have grown up believing that blood is thicker than water and that to walk away from family is one of the greatest sins on Earth.

I see those women who lose themselves almost entirely when they become mothers; either trying desperately to avoid judgement and keep up with the social stereotypes and conditions that try to convince them of everything a mother must be. Or giving every ounce of their time and energy to a child because this is the first time they have ever felt that truly transcendent experience of love that reminds them there is more to life.

And I feel for those who become so connected to a teacher or mentor that they stick with them long after the relationship has ceased to be of benefit to them, continuing to support those mentors as if indebted to them, even as they are being restricted and kept small.

None of those relationships in themselves are bad; and indeed, the choice to devote yourself to, keep looking for, or persist with any kind of relationship is not in itself a negative one. But when the intention behind any relationship is to give up rather than give of yourself, or when that devotion, searching or persisting becomes detrimental to you and your own sense of self, that is anything but positive.

I say this as someone who has taken that less than positive approach to many relationships, particularly when it comes to friends and romance.

I wrote earlier about the time I spent consciously single after a series of pretty disastrous romantic relationships; relationships I threw myself into wholly, even when that affection and energy wasn't returned or even respected. For years I lived in the shadows of wounding those relationships had left upon me, allowing myself to believe I was somehow deserving of unhappiness in love, while the relationships I experienced became more and more unhappy. It's something I see so often with clients too – incredible women who have convinced themselves they are somehow unworthy of the kind of respect and support that real partnership can bring, so instead settle for any old relationship, as long as it means they don't have to be alone.

Of course that always causes problems; relationships of that kind will only ever perpetuate the "not enough" whispers that live within us and continue our journey down a path of relationships that make us feel lonelier within them than we do without until the moment we choose to stop, to step away and look within ourselves instead of pointing a finger at the assortment of "losers" and "arseholes" and dreamy old "could have beens" we leave in our wake.

In many ways our heteronormative, sex and romance-obsessed culture encourages us to dwell on those past experiences, and to keep searching for the right person without ever taking the time to turn inwards and ask what that really means for us. And so my search continued for the longest time in all the wrong places; searching for the men who seemed to offer the relationships I thought would be good for me rather than those I actually wanted or needed for myself. Then giving and doing everything I could to turn myself into the person who was right for those relationships once in them, only to find myself broken-hearted and feeling that I was somehow lacking, when they inevitably ended badly.

I remember vividly, the ex-boyfriend who turned up to our second date late, drunk and without his wallet, not even questioning who would pay when we ordered dinner and leaving me wondering what the joke was as he got louder and more raucous as the night went on. Looking back now – hell, even looking back eighteen months later when we broke up, I wondered why I had even agreed to another date, never mind stuck with the guy for well over a year, even as our relationship became more and more one-sided. But the truth was that my inner teenage geek had – as she so often did in relationships back then – come out to play that night; convincing me that I was the boring one, that I should relax about the lateness, and possibly worst of all, that I should be grateful enough for this guy's company to more than willingly pay for dinner outright and put up with his bad jokes and awful behaviour throughout the rest of the night. The trend of that relationship continued, yet somehow I convinced myself to stick with it – terrified that at 32, I was too old to meet someone new and this might well be my very last chance at kids and happiness.

Thinking back I shudder, and want to wrap myself back then up in a warm, cosy blanket, as I tell her just how much more she deserves, and how much better a fit there is for her – and for him – out there, if only she will take the time to figure out what that truly means for her instead. In the days immediately after that relationship ended, I emailed him (something that makes me cringe right down to the soles of my feet as I remember it!) asking if we could give it another try. I will never forget his response – that he missed me but, "I just can't tell whether that's actually because I want to be with you or because I'm so used to having you around that you've become a habit." Brutal right? Albeit also unsurprisingly thoughtless, given what you already know about our early dates! However, that email also taught me a valuable lesson, because it turned out he was right. Like so many unpleasant relationships, ours had become so familiar that it felt safer to continue unhappily, than it did to walk away. But when I did walk away, closing that email and choosing to move forward towards a relationship that was more home than habit, the relief was palpable.

Of course that doesn't begin to describe the challenging relationships that happen within families too – ones that can be even more difficult to extricate ourselves from. Although I am fortunate to have a wonderful family, many of whom I would comfortably choose to spend time with, not everyone can say the same. And those are dynamics I have seen play out again and again in therapy sessions over the years, supporting a client through the painful process of recognising that their childhood was not only far from the stereotype of white picket-fenced happiness they have been told they *should* have had, but of working through the painful experiences they had instead, before potentially choosing to walk away from one or more family members once and for all.

We hear a lot about abusive relationships, but so often we consider those as only being within romantic partnerships. That can be the case, of course, but there are no limits to the relationships that can become abusive. Today there is a lot of talk about the empath and narcissist relationship, and understandably so. I've had more than a few clients who have suffered through such a relationship and are, years after, trying to deal with the wounds inflicted upon them through it.

Hell, I've been there, although in my case it was a friendship. A close enough friendship that I believed every time she told me I was in the wrong. I trusted the gaslighting enough to be convinced that I was a selfish, awful person long after I had realised those judgments had very little to do with me and more than a little to do with the other person's need for control.

For anyone who isn't sure what those terms mean, they refer to challenging and often abusive relationships which play out between two people on opposite sides of the empathetic spectrum. An empath is someone who tends to be attuned to other people's emotions and feels those deeply. They are naturally drawn to help and support others, but without an understanding of their own superpower for empathy, can easily find themselves feeling drained, overwhelmed or taken for granted. Narcissists, meanwhile, are almost the opposite. Although they often can read other people's feelings, they choose not to pay attention to those, unless for their own benefit, meaning they have a tendency to manipulate and to use those around them, in order to fulfil their own agenda. For narcissists, empaths make the perfect companions because they care so deeply, and often look to others for reassurance they don't carry within themselves. But of course that is incredibly dangerous for the empath who can find themselves drained, doubting themselves and so much more. This is a complex subject, and one that whole books have been written about, but is also one that it's important we are all aware of – especially those of us sensitive to others' thoughts and feelings.

However there is a problem with all of this talk about narcissists and empaths, in that it brings us into another potentially dangerous duality; the kind where we see one side of the coin as "good" and the other as intrinsically "bad." But so many narcissistic tendencies develop in response to trauma... And while true narcissistic personality disorder is something very specific in itself, those tendencies are things that can flare up in all of us from time to time and must be worked with and through to keep them in check.

Another issue I have with this focus on the empath and narcissist relationship is the idea of the empath as some sort of weak, perpetual victim. It's easy to think that, based on what you read online, but it's just not true. Being an empath is a real strength... Just as soon as we learn how to use those deep empathic feelings to trust and care for ourselves as much as we do for other people – more than we do at times when we make the decision to walk away from those relationships we know to be damaging to us.

As we in the West open up more and more to the spiritual sides of life, what makes some of these relationships even harder to deal with is the depth of history we have together. Not just in our current lives but in those that pull to us in meditation, healing sessions and through those unmistakable pulls of our souls when we meet someone we are inexplicably drawn to. Having journeyed with my own soul's story for many years, this is something I am all too familiar with, having engaged in friendships and other relationships time and time again because I had seen those people in a soul memory and assumed that meant we were somehow meant to be connected.

Memories like that of an ex-boyfriend, who I saw in lifetime after lifetime during my early days of working with past lives. I saw us working together in Atlantis, married in the early days of a life in late 18th century New Orleans and together again in the early 1900s. So of course I thought we were meant to be together – isn't that what all of the books tell you, after all? And so I put up with literally years of manipulation, discomfort and pain in the certainty that surely it would all come good! It took an incredible tarot reader who told me in no uncertain terms that, "This man is a soulmate yes, but that doesn't mean he is the person you're meant to be with. It means that he has things to teach you and vice versa. This is not forever," to make me stop and think. Although I'm sorry to say that even that wasn't enough to change my mind once and for all; instead spending another two years going back and forth in a relationship that made me feel less and less confident, before I eventually walked away.

What so many of the stories about soulmates and twin flames fail to tell us about recurring relationships though, is just how many of the relationships we are drawn to tend to be karmic – opportunities for us to connect again with a soul we have a difficult history with, in the hope of smoothing out the karma between us and resolving our issues. Unfortunately sometimes, no matter how persistent we are and how much we try, that karmic wound will not be worked out this time and will only ever deepen. In that case, our job is not to convince another person to consider their own karma differently, not even to try and force them to make changes, but to look after ourselves, knowing that we can only do what we can do in support of our own soul's progress, and that another person's choices are always up to them.

Let me say something simply and clearly: no-one is entitled to your time and your energy, unless that is something they are willing to return. And whatever your history or hopes of a future, any relationship that asks you to sacrifice everything that you are is not worth your while, no matter what you have been told or how much you think otherwise.

The independent life

With all of that said, it can be easy to think that life would be easier and less painful if it were lived largely alone. I have always been pretty independent and something of an introvert – living alone for a large part of my adult life, choosing to travel the world solo when I got the chance to take the trip of a lifetime, and being pretty damned self-sufficient in many ways. But after the end of the friendship I mentioned earlier, I made a real effort to step back from every relationship that offered potential danger. Which, in a world where we can never wholly predict another person's actions, meant almost every relationship outside of my family. I was hurt, afraid and no longer trusted myself to make safe decisions about those I let into my life. So there and then, I made the choice to close some doors.

As I began my consciously single period, I also stepped back from friends, keeping those I already knew at arm's length as far as possible and putting up the kind of brick wall boundaries that made it hard for anyone new to get too close. Initially, that period of time brought some benefits. It gave me the opportunity to give back to myself after years of over-giving to so many of the people around me, and allowed me to turn inwards and focus on my own healing and self-awareness, at a time when I had become so enmeshed in my connection to another person that I barely knew who I was anymore.

And let's be honest, it was also quiet, safe and in many ways easy to do exactly as I pleased, while letting in only those who had proven themselves over and over again to be trustworthy and were highly unlikely to hurt me.

I am a firm believer in independence; as I've mentioned elsewhere in this book. I believe that one of the most powerful and important things any of us can ever do is come back home to ourselves. Not in that cheesy way that means candlelit bubble baths and facemasks every night (unless that's what works for you!), but in the way I encourage at the start of every podcast episode – and at the start of this book – when I invite you to ask how you *really* are and then tune in to listen to the answer.

No-one else can ever know what it is like to live life as you. Or be able to feel every one of your emotions and see inside every corner of your brain, which means that no-one else has the opportunity to know and understand you as fully as you do yourself. Given that it's that knowledge and understanding that gives us the wisdom to make the best decisions for ourselves, as we move through life, why in the hell wouldn't we want to invest time and energy in it?

In Glennon Doyle's *Untamed*, she writes: "Self-love means that I have a relationship with myself built on trust and loyalty...I'll disappoint everyone else before I'll disappoint myself. I'll forsake all others before I'll forsake myself. Me and myself: we are till death do us part." For me this is the crux of it. What I gained from my time alone and what I would encourage every other person in the world to cultivate for themselves too... Albeit, perhaps not as dramatically as I did.

Because that time of life was also a lonely one; one in which the world went on around me while my own life seemed to stall. I saw friends having new experiences, meeting new people and trying new things, all while I felt like I was on a self-imposed lockdown long before Covid made it trendy. For every social occasion I turned down out of tiredness or a need to re-connect with myself, there was another that gave me FOMO, as I realised what a good time everyone else seemed to be having. And that left me wishing I'd just bitten back my fear and gotten involved.

What I learned was that in stopping trusting other people enough to have a place in my life, I wasn't loving myself but letting myself down; deeply doubting my ability to make the right decisions about where to invest my time and energy for starters. But also putting more burdens on myself than any of those past unhappy relationships had ever dared to do. Even now, years later, I know when I am becoming overwhelmed with the world because I'll tend to retreat inwards – far further than I know is comfortable – and refuse to reach out to other people for help or support, choosing instead to carry all the burdens of life by myself.

That's exhausting – as exhausting as being in a painfully co-dependent relationship – and also hugely unhelpful. As awesome as we all are, none of us have all of the answers, and everyone needs a little support from time to time.

Fortunately amongst it all were a handful of friendships – some new into my life and some much older. Friends who point blank refused to allow me to go solo, nudging at those high boundaries of mine just enough to make the top bricks tumble down, so they could see over and see for themselves the corner I had backed myself into.

Those friends were the kind of people willing to put in the extra effort with me in those early days as you would with a rescue animal: paying extra attention to me and my moods, treading gently so as not to spook me and supporting me in ways I hadn't even realised I wanted or needed, until I learned that I could trust them enough to open up and to give back in return.

Will those friendships last a lifetime? I sure hope so, but the truth is that none of us know how much of our lives anyone other than ourselves will be present for. That can be a terrifying thought, I know, one that can send people even further into a place of fear-fuelled independence than I found. But in a world where so much beauty can be found in connections of all kinds, we must remember that fierce independence – for all of its many powers and benefits – can only go so far before it becomes detrimental to us and to the world.

Flying the flag for interdependence

So often we are taught about a model for relationships of all kinds that is, when we truly examine it, unhealthy; asking us to rely solely on one another to the point of co-dependence or expecting us to sacrifice ourselves wholly for the benefit of another person simply as a sign that we care. That isn't right, and I firmly believe it to be a long, long way from the balanced world that we are trying to build.

But as we've discussed above and elsewhere in this book under the heading of individualism; any in-balance world also needs to take us far from the place of ferocious or enforced independence that sees us unable to care for or be cared for by another person; a state that so many people have experienced with devastating results.

The key here, always? Learning how to form interdependent relationships of all kinds.

Interdependent relationships aren't adjoined units in which two people operate as one, but are instead teams supporting one another to be all that they can be while each playing their part and supported to shine their own unique lights along the way.

They are spaces of trust, rather than reliance, in which we can offer and look to one another for support as it is needed. But recognise the need for balance and flow within that, without ever simply expecting another person to meet our needs.

They are relationships built on care, respect and love for another person, not on possession over that person, their time or their energy no matter what.

They are experiences of flow, which we know will change over time – sometimes bringing us closer together and at others drawing us further apart, but knowing throughout it all, that a true interdependent relationship can trust in its foundations.

And they are connections in which we are allowed to be ourselves; wholly and utterly ourselves, without needing to diminish our light, hide our fundamental beliefs or be anything more or less than the perfectly imperfect humans that we are. A state that will inevitably, despite our best interests, cause us to hurt people in our lives and cause us to be hurt by them, but which provides the opportunity for us to face up to and communicate those hurts in a way that enables everyone involved to heal, to recover and to rebuild moving forwards.

Of course, not every relationship will be alike. With over 7 billion unique people on this planet, no two relationships should or will ever be exactly the same, and so there is no right or wrong model for a relationship of any sort. But an awareness of interdependence – the ability to be independent together – is a good place to start.

I say start, because I recognise that it's also not as easy as suggesting that every relationship can move immediately into a place of interdependence. This is a long and challenging journey, even for those of us who are unpicking the relationship patterns that have been drummed into us for centuries. This involves unpacking the wounds we have picked up as a result, and figuring out exactly how to rebuild in the way that is right for us. But we must also accept that not everyone will choose to take such a journey for themselves.

That means that not all of our relationships can become interdependent, including some of those nearest and dearest to our hearts. That can sound like a red flag, and maybe in some cases it is, but that doesn't have to be the case. This is not an instruction to sack off every relationship with someone who is unwilling to look at and change their own patterns of behaviour.

Only you can decide what is right for you. Only you can choose who gets to be in your life, what is important for those relationships and how much energy they involve. Only you can choose the ways you enforce those choices, and the extent to which you allow anything outside of them to slide with any individual at any given time.

The Ninth Key: BOUNDARIES

The kind of relationships that are built upon a foundation of interdependence require trust, respect and confidence for sure – all things that need to be built over time. However, there is one thing that can really help us with the rebalancing of our relationships: boundaries.

We are entitled to have boundaries within our relationships. What's more, it is healthy to have boundaries within our relationships if we want to maintain our energy, let the people we are closest to know what is and is not acceptable behaviour for us, and ensure we know the same for them too.

A boundary can be anything from no looking at one another's phones without express permission, to no turning up unannounced at a person's house, unless it is an absolute emergency and a billion other things in between. Our boundaries are often as unique as the relationships that they are made for.

As a therapist, boundaries are something that are vital to my work. They tell clients what they can expect from me and also let them know what I expect in return, ensuring that our work stays on track for its original purpose and keeping us both safe and supported at every turn. In those cases, the boundaries are very clear and linked to our work together; talking about the limitations of our work together, about the expectation of confidentiality between us, and about what will happen if we need to contact one another between sessions, for example. Of course things are different when it comes to personal relationships, but that's not to say we shouldn't have boundaries.

One of my most important friendships became so much stronger when we had a conversation about the fact that when one of us is in a place of anxiety or overwhelm, we would be unable to hold space for the other. We agreed that, if all we could offer on some days and in some situations was a message containing a heart, then that didn't mean we didn't love one another, but simply that someone else would need to pick this one up because we were unable to.

To figure out our boundaries, we must first take the time to understand what we need in order to feel safe with and supported by the people in our lives; as well as how and where we are best able to support them too. In order for those boundaries to come into their own, we must also communicate them. And that is where this can be tough... Another of my closest friendships changed drastically when, after a message conversation in which we had unintentionally overstepped one another's boundaries by giving unwanted or asked for opinions, insensitive to situations the other person was trying to work through on their own, my friend picked up the phone and Facetimed me. While it was super scary – even for us as full grown adults – to have the sort of conversation that was about apologising and understanding how better to support one another in future, that conversation also felt like a huge step forwards for our friendship, since which we have been honest with one another and have really come to learn more about where we can and cannot show up for each other.

This idea of setting boundaries with another person is rarely about pinning a piece of paper to a noticeboard declaring that this is a hard line which must not and cannot ever be crossed; although sometimes there may be things that are that clear and need to be shared almost that directly!

More often though, our boundaries are things which flow, changing from relationship to relationship, situation to situation and changing over time too. I have very different boundaries during the days I am bleeding each month, for example, than those when I am ovulating, because that is what I need at those times of the month. Meanwhile, if you have a close personal relationship with a colleague, for example, then the boundaries of your relationship may well be very different in the workplace to those you have at home. That doesn't make either wrong, it just means that you both have different needs in each facet of your relationship.

And that word both is an important part of why that noticeboard I mentioned earlier is unlikely to be an effective way to agree boundaries with another person, because this conversation often needs to be a collaborative one that we agree with another person rather than for them. That's not to say that you need to change your own boundaries based on the opinion of anyone in your life, but it is to see that every interdependent relationship is based on a foundation of mutual respect and understanding.

When we make the setting of boundaries a conversation rather than a declaration we have to explain what is not OK for us. And that can be tough – particularly when we have been so heavily conditioned to have boundaryless relationships of all kinds. But we also show that we respect and value the other person enough to explain to them why this is important to us and give them the opportunity to say whether that is something they can accept or not.

EXERCISES AND PROMPTS

MEDITATION

Journeying with boundaries: Working with images and feelings, we will journey together with your boundaries; what they mean to you and where and how you can implement them to stay safe in all ways.

RITUAL

Union with self: Best carried out at the time of the Full Moon, this ritual offers you the opportunity to make a commitment to yourself in your power and wholeness.

EXERCISES

- Visualise yourself with energetic cords of light coming out of you to all of the people you are connected to. What do those cords look like? Which ones look healthy and/or feel good? And which look less so?

  Of the second batch, consider which you would like to tend and how you could do that, then consider which it's time to let go of. Visualise yourself with a giant pair of scissors or a sword as you snip those cords in the highest good.

- Think about the boundaries you would like or need to set with important people in your life. Are these conversations you could have? I invite you to do that if and where it feels right.

JOURNAL PROMPTS

- Which are and have been the most positive relationships in your life? What was it about those relationships that made them so good?

- Equally which are and have been your most challenging relationships? What was it about them which made that the case?

- What do you need from relationships of all kinds in order to feel safe and supported and to have your needs met?

- What do you bring to your relationships?

- Where relationships in your life have ended – for good or bad – consider why that was and what you learned from those experiences. How do or would you approach your relationships differently as a result?

WISDOM

EMOTION   LOGIC

We have already mentioned those voices of the head and heart; the ones that will demand to be heard – sometimes in direct opposition to one another – whenever the time comes to make a decision. Studies have proven that the tissue in the brain and the heart is almost identical, which adds to the belief that both have important insights to share, but it can be hard to know how to choose which to listen to.

Then of course we talk about our intuition, which lives in neither head nor heart but can certainly influence both. However, to allow those three sources of our inner wisdom to unite and guide us effectively, we need to be able to get out of our own way and rebuild our connection with and trust in all three of them, particularly in a world that talks so disparagingly about one of them.

You know what I mean here; the ways our head – the rational, fact-based voice within us is the one to be taken seriously and followed before anything else rather than our heart – that emotional, silly voice that should receive eye rolls and a condescending pat on the head.

It was years before I realised this in itself is a feminist issue; years that had culminated in two periods of antidepressant use, a great deal of being laughed at and told to be sensible, and one relationship in which my boyfriend took great pleasure in calling me a "psycho."

Understanding the fluctuations of my own emotions is possibly the biggest gift I received through tracking my menstrual cycle. It taught me that for around 20 days of each month my moods are relatively even and are generally related to whatever is going on around me day-to-day (with a tendency towards anxiety if I've stepped into that place of overdoing).

Then there are two days where I am anxious AF. Where I worry about everything I've said, everything others have – or haven't – said and when, if that anxiety is left unchecked, it will Run. The. Show. Even more so in the parts of my life where I am feeling less than happy or secure.

For two days a month I have a low mood that borders on depressive with the feeling that nothing in the world makes sense. These are the days when I want to do nothing but read romance novels, binge cheesy Netflix shows and dream of a different life.

And then there are the giddy days; those that feel great when I'm in them but can often see me agreeing to more than I'm comfortable with. I can't tell you how many times I have agreed to social occasions on those handful of giddy days, or overbooked my schedule saying, "Aah it'll be fine, I'll have the energy," only to later curse myself for how out of line with my energy levels those plans are.

For the longest time, I thought and felt as though this was wrong, that I should somehow be able to transcend all of the things I felt on any given day and live from a permanent state of static, logical thinking. That's what our cognicentric world wants from us, right? Logic and rationality. But to go down that path is to miss out on so much; so much beauty, so much wonder, and the true power of our emotion.

Feeling the feels

The word emotion comes from the old French word "émouvoir" which means to stir up or agitate. That's a good description of the power our emotions hold, not to mention the reasons we're so often told to suppress and mistrust them.

Think about the times you've been drained of energy only to have something incredible happen which lit up your heart and gave you the boost you needed to carry you through the day. Equally, how about the times the opposite has happened – you've been powering through the day, feeling like the Sun was shining upon you, only to have a piece of bad news that floored you. Our emotions are so often our fuel, the things that power us forward or pull us backwards. For us to be operating at best possible capacity, we need our emotions to be in full and balanced flow just as much as our physical bodies.

There is a lot of talk in the world today about purpose, and equal amounts of criticism for that term. For what is purpose? Is it a job, starting a business? Many out there would say yes, and more some would even tell you that purpose must involve creating something brand new; bucking the norms of society to do something different than what has been done before. But to say that, is to miss the point. It is to tell us that purpose must be linked to income. The two are not always synonymous. True purpose is both more complex and much more simple, and our emotions are so often the signposts that lead us there.

Our greatest joys pull us in the direction we're headed. But not only our joys, our anger too. In her Divine Feminine Oracle, Meggan Watterson talks about the idea of sacred rage; that fury that burns within and spills out of us when we see an injustice we cannot sit back and ignore. Our hearts are only truly stirred by that which is important to us, that's why we follow them.

What if you were to fill your life with more of what lights up your heart; to take action on more of the things that enrage or break it, where would that lead you? Maybe into paid work that was aligned with those things yes – and one day in whatever sacred economy lies ahead of us almost certainly. But that doesn't have to happen right now. Right now those things may be the passions you devote time to outside of work, and those in which you feel most at one with yourself. Whatever we choose to do with them, if we can find the places where our passions intersect then we find a path to what is right – maybe not in the sense of being true and factual for the whole world, but certainly in terms of our own meaning. But first we must learn to listen to and interpret those emotions.

Maybe this is where the most challenging aspect of this comes into play; in learning to listen to our emotions, without being carried away and overwhelmed by them.

That can happen so easily, our emotions overtaking us like some sort of storm or tsunami. As an aside, so can our thoughts – maybe that's why anxiety is so prevalent in a society that puts so much stead in the mental. We have all been in that place of giddiness I mentioned earlier, where we say or do things we later regret simply because we're so excited. Equally, we have all lost our temper over something that was more a symptom than a cause of our anger, only to cause unnecessary problems for ourselves further down the line.

In many ways our emotions are like the elements themselves; vital building blocks that are so necessary in our lives. But if left untended and allowed to go out of balance, they can cause chaos and destruction.

We tend those emotions like we do anything else – by regularly taking the time and space to get to know them and understand what they need. By doing that, we notice as they start to rise, so that we can pay attention to the whispers of their early warning signs rather than wait until they explode into a shout. Once we recognise those subtleties, we can get to know and understand the emotions themselves.

What are those emotions really saying? Listen long and deep enough and they will begin to make perfect sense. That's how we learn where our emotions are leading us, rather than being distracted by anything and everything that happens along the way.

There is a downside to keeping those emotions in balance though – something that our society has, for so long, tried its damnedest to keep us away from. Meaning that if we want to get in touch with these things, we have to face our emotions – all of them – and feel them in their fullness.

Feeling is something that this world is so desperate to keep us from, probably because it helps us break out of the bonds that prevent us from connecting with the deeper meaning of our lives. Arguably, that is exactly why so much of our capitalist society encourages us to numb – to look outside of ourselves not only for wisdom but for the kind of soothing that keeps our emotions at bay, rather than feel and act upon them.

It tells us what we should get angry at through the news agenda that gives us clear good and bad guys. It invites us to drink a bottle of wine or a cocktail if we need to relax, to eat sugar as a treat that will make everything feel better, to work to give us purpose and meaning, and to lust after and devote ourselves to another person in order to feel happy.

We are told that emotions are things to be soothed and settled, and that the way to do that is to spend money. Money we inevitably have to work to earn.

The problem with that strategy is that it eventually disconnects us from so many of our emotions, and so much of what they have to offer.

Time to share more of my own story. A few years back I went through what was emotionally the toughest time of my life; within one year my dad became ill, I had two break ups; we had two deaths in the family; a close friendship began to crumble and I found myself faced with a work situation that can only be called abusive; all while pursuing the dream of having my first book published and re-training as a therapist. I was constantly sad, angry and frustrated.

Midway through the year, I decided enough was enough. I couldn't and wouldn't deal with any of the pain I was feeling, a pain that not only physically hurt but also made it so bloody difficult to do the work that felt so important and necessary for someone with bills to pay. And so, like the vampires in The Vampire Diaries (yes, that is my second reference to that show!), I switched off my feelings.

I went from being someone who was in love with so much of nature and laughed until her belly hurt at least once a week, while also sobbing herself to the point of dehydration just as regularly, to someone who just... didn't. Not unless she was too drunk to stop those feelings spilling out.

In years past I had, like so many of us, often searched for validation outside of myself. But by cutting off my emotions, I developed a complete inability to recognise or trust the way I felt about anything, especially myself. Instead, all I trusted in was hitting the targets I was set at work – even those that made me uncomfortable; attention from men – even those who made me feel sick; and asking for and receiving guidance from others.

I couldn't trust my own inner wisdom because I had disconnected myself from the very language it spoke. And even when I decided it was time to tune into my feelings again, that language was one I'd almost forgotten to speak. It took work to reconnect. Difficult, uncomfortable work.

For me, that meant many of the things I've mentioned before; sobriety, two years with no dating, walking away from people and situations that were no good for me, a lot of hermitting and a serious investment in therapy. That took me first to a place where I stopped pretending that drunken tears and the buzz of excitement over a new guy texting me were the wholeness of my feelings, and then supported me to face up to the scary, shitty depths of what my feelings truly were and could be.

That wasn't just the obviously painful emotions, but also those you would think I'd be happy to dive into. Earlier we spoke of the links between love and fear, and it's hard to tell this story without also mentioning the link between love and grief. When I tapped into my feelings, I began to remember those joyful experiences and beautiful memories that had been dulled out in my quest to numb the pain of grief – memories I was absolutely heartbroken to let go of. That heartbreak was enough to make me cry and rage until I feared I would never stop. But I did stop; and that's when my emotions settled into a language I could speak.

Logic

Undoubtedly, many of the reasons our society has become so cerebrally focussed is because logic is safe.

Logic is the thing that prevents heartbreak because when we rely on rationality and fact, we will rarely be heartbroken. For when something is based solely on fact and the rational, not only will it be safe from the disappointment of true emotion, but it will also bring us a deeper understanding of how to create more certainty.

Of course, today we have taken that too far. We trust rationality over all else to the point that emotion is considered foolish. Particular emotions are considered dangerous and at least half of the population have been encouraged to disconnect from their emotions completely. You know what I mean here, the way in which women – especially Black and Trans women – are vilified for their emotions, and the ways that those who identify as men are mocked for theirs. We have genuinely reached a point in some parts of society where it is considered more normal for a man to attack someone than to speak about their emotions.

In many ways, I wonder if our reliance on logic was a way of recovering from the pain inflicted upon us by our changing beliefs and blind following of religion. Yet we find ourselves at a time when many people have come to put all of their faith in logic with the same blinkered perspective.

I was once called out on Instagram as being a "snake oil peddling charlatan" for posting a quote by Markus Almond, which read:

> "I believe I have a soul because I have smelled the first day of spring and I have listened to Aretha Franklin on vinyl. And the things I feel in those moments cannot be explained by science."

I know, beautiful. And pretty innocuous words right? Yet someone was so offended by the idea of science not being able to explain everything that they chose to name call.

Not everything is logical – the passions we are drawn to, the things that ignite our sacred rage and the individual callings of each of our beings. Some of our responses are purely emotion-based or maybe even transcend that emotion, just as they do logic. To pretend otherwise is to ignore so much of the experience of life. And while doing so may cut us off from the pain of disappointment or heartbreak, it also keeps us from so much of the opposite – from pure joy, hope and maybe even wisdom.

None of this is to say that logic is all bad. Just as that outer knowledge that comes through science and academia gives us so much insight into the world, logic can also provide us with a much-needed viewpoint.

Often it's logic that tempers the flames of our emotions into a place where we can move forwards without being overwhelmed. What's more, often it's logic that gives us the "how" of that movement. If you are an activist for example, you can take action to stand up for the causes that most touch your heart and passions, but it's the logic of organising that really enables that activism to make a difference.

Our emotions are the colour of who we are. Our logic is the framework that enables us to follow that colour and look after ourselves in the process.

I mentioned earlier that so much of what I lost myself in during my own dark night of the soul was work, because I needed to pay the bills – don't we all? And although I can't tell you what will happen in any future economies, right now I struggle to see any in which we won't need some form of logic, even if that is just to work out how to do what needs doing.

Where emotion has so much to offer us individually, logic is something that we can, usually, agree on collectively. Logic is the place where our emotions find compromise with one another; the point where we can truly move forwards together. As physical beings, logic is so often something we need, in order to ensure our basic needs are met – together and separately. Without logic we may well forget to eat, drink water, or to do so many of the other things needed to keep us going. Without logic we wouldn't know how to move forwards – individually or together. Maybe logic is something that enables us to be physical beings in this human world.

But a problem with logic is that it is not always infallible. Just as research can be conducted with any individual agenda, those with extreme viewpoints will always find ways to support their beliefs with logic – often in ways they share more and more broadly until it is considered to be "common sense" and accepted as fact, without question. So many of those so-called facts can be limited at best –

even as I write this I recognise how caught up I am in the bounds of logic, thinking about how the book is structured and how to pay the bills – and dangerous at worst, particularly when they are adopted without context.

The wisdom within

Even knowing the benefits and challenges of both our head and heart voices, there are times when the two can come into conflict with one another and leave us completely confused as to which we should follow.

What makes that even more complex is the inclusion of a third voice – the intuition or soul voice that we are so often told is most trustworthy of all. And understandably so. I guess, our intuition is a voice loaded with insight which often surpasses so much of what you consciously know. However, that is not to say that voice will give everything you need, or that we should ever beat ourselves up for choosing not to follow it. After all, where is the learning and freewill in that?

In truth, each of the voices within us holds insight into the answers we seek. But none of them hold everything on their own; a lesson I learned the hard way after making a few bad decisions based solely on my head, my heart or maybe even my intuition.

For a long time, I believed that meant I couldn't trust myself to make a decision at all; something that left me feeling completely stuck, unable to move forwards in fear of making a "wrong" decision and finding myself miserable or disappointed. Instead the stuckness that created left me feeling... well, miserable and inevitably disappointed too, when I realised just how many opportunities I kept missing thanks to my refusal to make a decision. But still, that feeling seemed safer than trying to reconnect with the inner guidance I had lost all faith and trust in.

Until one day I realised I had never been listening to myself fully – I had been listening only to *parts* of myself.

Earlier, I suggested that our emotions are the signposts that tell us what is true for us, while logic gives us insight into the how of that – what is safe and practical for us. Intuition adds to the equation by telling us what will get us closer to wherever it is that we are meant to be in this life and what will take us further away. But even with all of those different facets, these voices together still don't tell us everything we need. To get that, we must look to our wisdom.

Yes, wisdom. A word that can seem so incredibly intangible and difficult to attain in a world that gives us ample pathways for knowledge and experience, but no time or space – arguably the vital ingredients in this process – to fully process either, leading us to believe that wisdom is something we can only find in other people.

But that's simply not true. Although other people may have wisdom of their own, which is always useful to listen to and learn from them, but the wisdom that truly matters in our own lives doesn't come directly from anyone else.

That's not to say that wisdom is something easily born within us either, although that is the place where it begins to emerge.

Wisdom comes when we allow the inner and outer knowledge we have already talked about to come together with our emotions, logic, intuition, experience, learnings, the teachings of other people and the realisations we have had along the way. When all of those things are brought together and brewed within our inner alchemical cauldron, that's when they are finally able to become more than the sum of their parts. That is when wisdom is born.

I know, this sounds complicated and it can be. But the very nature of that alchemical process often means that it is anything but complex too. Often it means that our hefty quests in pursuit of wisdom are precisely the opposite of what we actually need to do, and that wisdom itself will hit us at exactly the moment we least expect it.

We have all had those moments within our own journeys through life where we have struggled with a concept or idea for the longest time; reading all of the books, watching all of the videos and even having all of the conversations with other people on a particular subject. All while feeling as though we were obviously missing a trick because whatever subject they were talking about made no sense at all to us.

A brilliant example of this comes from a lengthy and repeated conversation I had recently with a good friend on the subject of love. It was a topic she was struggling with, one that brings with it so many societally conditioned ideas and so many personal experiences that can between them inevitably lead us to start wondering, "What even is love?" No matter how many books my friend read on the subject, or how many opinions she canvassed (including mine – that love is a state we can flow within both with and without another person), this was a question she continually struggled with. Then one day after a long hike, she sent me a message: "I get it! I was walking today and it just clicked – love doesn't have to be about another person. It's just like you said, and just like I'd read. It didn't make sense before, but in that moment it all fell into place."

That isn't as weird as it sounds. Wisdom cannot be conjured up on demand but takes time to stew and grow. That's probably why it is usually most associated with older people and, in the context of Goddess worship, with the archetype of the Crone.

The Crone is one of the most feared figures in society; not only because she is a woman who defies all expectations and is happy to live outside of the norms of society, but also because her greatest power is something that so many in our busy, always-on cultures have neither the time nor the space to cultivate and grow for themselves. But I wonder how much of that power we would have access to, if only we were to take our cues from the Crone and take the time and space for ourselves to process and alchemise all that we consciously and unconsciously know.

In the years since my own period of indecision, I've learned an important lesson about how to sort through the longings, wants, shoulds and could haves in my mind, in order to return to a bigger picture view of what is the right way forward for me. But I've also learned the vital ingredient that comes after this, when I give myself the time to sit with a big decision, wherever possible, and allow space for wisdom to arrive, and to use all of my senses to connect with it when that happens.

The Tenth Key: CONNECTION

Our Western obsession with dualities likes to split our inner knowing and feelings into parts, fixating on which parts of ourselves we should and shouldn't trust most of all, and how we go about doing that. But even to talk about the different voices within us is, in many ways, missing a pretty critical element: That they are all you.

If you have ever looked at a large diamond, you will undoubtedly have noticed that the stone looks different from every angle; each facet giving off a slightly different shine or portraying an additional detail we might otherwise have missed. Yet no matter which way you look at it, you will always be looking at the very same diamond comprised of the very same materials and parts.

While some of our facets may have been clouded by the dirt of someone else's opinions, or had their shine dimmed by the lights the world shone upon us, once we really look within ourselves we begin

There are different facets of us with different views of the world – views it is important to get to know so that we can discern between them, and find common ground amongst them. All of those facets are a part of us. And it is only by re-connecting ourselves to those parts, and re-connecting them to one another, that we can truly begin to see the wisdom of our own selves and experiences.

What if we were to bring together our knowing, gut feelings, emotions, physical sensations and values and sit with them all until they were able to co-exist within one single united diamond of wisdom? Imagine if we were then to sit with ourselves in that place of re-connection and listen to each facet of ourselves, until we knew them so intimately that we could understand even the smallest of nudges from any of those warning systems.

Decisions would be easier to make. But wherever those decisions led us we would undoubtedly find it easier to deal with the consequences too, because we would also be fully connected with our wisdom, as it brewed and made itself known; a wisdom that would give us so much insight on ourselves and the world.

EXERCISES AND PROMPTS

MEDITATIONS

Meeting your wise inner guide: Just as the name says, this journey is all about connecting with – or reconnecting with – the wiser inner figure who is here to guide you from a place of your highest good.

Your embodied feelings: How and where do you feel your feelings? Use this visualisation to connect to those feelings within your physical body with the aim of recognising them more easily and understanding them further.

RITUAL

Invite in every part of yourself: It's time to reconnect with yourself more fully. This ritual invites back all of the wise, wonderful and powerful parts of you that may have become disconnected over the years.

EXERCISES

- What if you were to tune into your emotions and let them lead the way for a day, where would that lead you?

- What if you were to follow logic?

- What if you were to go about your days expressing different voices within you?

JOURNAL PROMPTS

- What do you know to be true for you and how do you know it?

- What is your relationship with each of the different facets of you?

  Emotion - Logic - Intuition

- What lights you up and what engages you? Why? Keep asking that.

- What are you passionate about – for good and bad?

- There is a famous quote that reads: "I sat with my anger long enough and it told me its name was grief." What would your feelings tell you if you sat with and spoke to them?

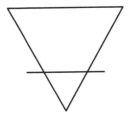

earth

The foundation of all. The place from which life springs anew and to which we all return.

Earth is the root of all, the support that keeps us grounded and steady.

Through Earth our needs are met. Through Earth all can be created, built and held firm; the sturdiness from and around which our lives are built.

We welcome the Earth in the North, in the dark of the night, the cold of Winter and the quiet wisdom of the aged Crone.

In Earth we rest our Body, the aches in its bones allowed to settle as they pause under shelter and fortify themselves for a new beginning.

With Earth come the fallen leaves, blanketed under the snow to fertilise the soil below,

And with Earth comes the safety of that we call home, supportive, warm and always the protector.

To forego Earth is to fly ungrounded, unrooted out of touch with oneself.

And to restrict Earth is to leave someone unsteady, without resource or rest.

But to leave Earth untended is to become stagnant and restricted, choking on vines as they chain you in place.

It is too afraid to move forward, to rise or to change, staying forever in the place we call safe.

But Earth is the fertility of beginnings, that comes with each ending. It gives it's all so that we may live safe and should take its place in balance.

So we call to the North and to Earth, to the depths of the night and the peace of Crone, to the death of Winter and the dark of the Moon.

We call to the trees and the flowers, to the animals and caves, to the sturdy roots, the rolling hills and the gnomes that make their homes in the woods.

And we ask them to join with us, to work with us and to bless us with their grounding, their sturdiness, their fertility and their abundance. And we take this step on our journey to sacred balance.

To the North and the Earth, hail and welcome.

May it be so.

To hear this invocation in full along with a short story, **The Tree at the Heart of the Earth,** visit the additional materials link at the back of the book.

CYCLICAL LIVING

LIFE   DEATH

I mentioned right at the start of this book the power that tracking my menstrual cycles brought me. The truth is that it changed everything. It made me understand myself and also explained the ways I understood the world.

We've been taught that life should be lived in accordance with those solar energies – always either on or off, with huge marker points at either side of that line and no shades of grey in between. But so much of that is forgetting the power and influence of lunar energy; the fact that while the Sun may be the force of all life, it's the Moon that controls so much of the rhythm of that life – of this Earth.

As we have talked about elsewhere, it's easy to think we have turned away from the Moon because it encourages rest – something our capitalist structures aren't huge fans of; or that we have been pulled in the direction of the Sun because of its ties to the God rather than the Goddess. It's even easy to think that we've been pulled toward the light of the Sun because we're afraid of the dark of the Moon.

None of that is wrong, but I would argue it goes deeper than all of those things. I would argue that to follow the light of the Moon is to willingly acknowledge, and maybe even surrender to the idea of death. In fact cyclical living of any sort, arguably, means to embrace the endings of our lives, just as we do the beginnings and the time in between.

Maybe that sounds paradoxical, but cyclical living is inevitably to live with one eye on dying. That sentence may trigger something in you. It may sound fatalistic, scary or even depressing. But I can tell you from experience, that it is also liberating. Let me explain.

Death as a transition

Dr Karl Albrecht wrote that there are five types of fear all humans have in common, the first being extinction or ceasing to exist. I guess that's why we all try so damned hard to create a legacy that can be left behind us. But it's also why we, as a race that have been told life is a simple A to B, are so damned terrified of death.

So terrified that every piece of media we consume tells us the worst thing that can happen to a person is the end of their physical life and that, even scarier still is the idea of what may come back and terrorise us (they almost always terrorise) from the unknown that lies beyond physical life.

I always remember reading a book by the medium, Gordon Smith, in which he wrote that people often asked why he was so cheery and optimistic. His response was always that he had learned death was nothing to be feared and after all, if there is nothing to fear in death then what is there to be afraid of?

Personally, I would say there's still a lot. But then, as a woman who is weirdly terrified of wooden popsicle sticks thanks to past life trauma, maybe I'm not the best person to ask!

However, I do understand what he's saying. For the longest time, my greatest fear was of losing the ones that I love. I vividly remember hitting that point all kids do when I realised that death comes to everyone and became terrified I would be left alone. Fast forward a few decades and personal experience of the searing pain that grief can bring, and I know how awful those losses can be. However, over 20 years of working with spirit and my own soul's journey has also shown me that there is more to death than endings.

I believe passionately that no-one should ever accept anything outright until they've had whatever proof they need for themselves, so this is not my attempt to convince you to believe anything. But personally I have had enough experiences to prove to me that there is life after death and our loved ones stay with us in one form or another after they have left their physical bodies. What's more, I've also had enough, evidence to firmly believe that we – and they – return to physical life time and time again in different places and different forms, all with different lessons to learn. With that in mind, I'm firmly of the belief that death itself isn't anything to be afraid of, no matter what the world might tell us.

I can't tell you exactly what happens when we die, and maybe this is part of the problem. That in a world which focusses so heavily on the tangible, the certain and the logical; a world that has led us all to believe we must always be in control; a state that exists outside of our living human comprehension is incredibly challenging for us to consider or understand.

I can tell you my favourite depiction of death though. It's a scene from a biopic about the medium James van Praagh which shows a man lying in a hospital bed surrounded by his loved ones. At the moment the man's life support machine turns off, the gathered family begin to weep. Meanwhile a dog bounds into the room and jumps up... onto the man who sits up to greet them, then follows the dog into a corridor where they are met by a crowd of beaming people. An ending of one existence but not an ending overall, simply a transition into a new way of being.

Physical death is not only our greatest mystery, but also the end of our human form and everything our conscious minds know. So is it any surprise many of those minds find it terrifying?

But if we step back, we recognise that not every death is a physical one, nor is it the permanent end of something. We see nature itself die off every year as the plants lose their flowers and shed the leaves they have worked so hard to grow in a blaze of glorious colours. And we experience deaths of a sort regularly throughout our lives, just as the Moon does every time we end a particular chapter or cycle and transition into something new. Yet still, even as we celebrate those transitions and the beauty they bring us, we refuse to see how they may apply within our own lives.

And this isn't just in the one-off changes or decisions either: we spend a fortune trying to slow down ageing so we can keep any reminder of physical death at bay; use electric lighting to eke out the last of the daytime and artificial temperature control to ensure we never have to deal with the extremes of nature. We even use the power of science to try and stop time and nature because we can. Without ever pausing to wonder whether we *should*, or what we may be missing out on in the process. Without ever pausing to question what effect a continual drive to embody life will do to and for us and our world, even as we see evidence of a natural world fighting so desperately for the rest, quiet and change of the other half of its cycle, that we can no longer hold back the wheel.

The problem with a culture that fears death is that every transition, and every possibility of loss will be considered something to be afraid of. It's why so many of us cling on to the status quo, no matter how painful, especially if we have no tangible view of the new beginnings that may lie ahead. Instead, we see only the endings that must be experienced first, endings that loom so large and terrifying when we are unable to see them as part of a continuous and more complex cycle.

With every chapter of this book I've written, I've found myself getting passionate and thinking, "This! This is the crux of Divine Feminism!" But with this one that might just be true.

By focussing on the linear rather than the cyclical, we have robbed ourselves of so much, abused ourselves and abused nature in so many ways. And for what? To try and avoid the most natural thing in this Universe, something that will come to us all eventually, no matter how hard we push against it.

What an awful lot of needless struggle.

Looking on the bright side of life

Let me assure you now that I don't believe life is all bad. In fact, if asked to describe myself, I will often use the label "lover of life" and while I don't fear death for myself I have no desire for it to come anytime soon; I have a lot of living to do first.

Life is our opportunity to experience and embrace everything this Earth has to offer, and while I don't claim to be able to solve the age-old question of its purpose, I do wholly believe it is always an incredible opportunity for us to expand, learn and grow.

That is inevitably something we're doing every single day. A few years ago, I remember starting a Twitter challenge to post something new I had learned each day for 100 days and the hardest part was never finding something, but instead trying to figure out how to cram each day's learnings into one tweet. A life lived with that eye on expanding our hearts, our minds and our awareness is an incredible thing, the problem is when we start to believe that expansion must be linear and constant.

Perhaps the reason cyclical living has become unheard of in our overwhelmingly capitalist world is its fundamental teaching that there is no such thing as a constant – no, even when it comes to expansion.

As we have discussed elsewhere, there will always be times in life when our energies are pulled inwards, not to act and grow, but to rest and process. And with that comes the recognition there are times when some aspects of life will flow incredibly easily while others will feel stuck and as immovable as a mountain.

I wrote earlier about the way my emotions fluctuate through the month, and as someone who menstruates it's probably no surprise that my physical body does the same. I love to swim, and there are times of the month that my body seems to glide through the water and can swim a mile without pausing to consider. Then there are others when I seem to drag myself through the water with limbs made of lead that can barely manage 500 metres. Once upon a time I would force myself to keep going on those days, determining that I wasn't making progress unless I was swimming further, faster and stronger each time. Yet that would only ever leave me feeling drained on those tougher days, with none of those post-exercise endorphins I was promised, anywhere to be found.

And it's not just the menstrual cycle that causes fluctuations. The more I've allowed my life to flow with my energies rather than push against them, the more I have realised how much more creative I am at certain times of the year, and how I do my best cleaning not in Spring as I'm told I should, but in late Autumn, when the world around me is focussed on releasing and letting go; how much this Libra rising gets a burst of productive energy in September, and how much she likes to hide away from the world in the final weeks before each birthday. I've learned to work with those things rather than against them, just as every other species on our planet lives their lives rather than trying to force itself into some sort of linear pattern that consists only of life, death and the in-between, with no nuance on what lies between or outside of those points.

But of course, much of our human world does operate within that linear structure, which tells us we must live a life of constancy, and there are practical reasons for that too, of course – kids can't be left to fend for themselves during January because Earth is hibernating and calling us to do the same. Even for me, someone who is self-employed and currently has no children to take care of, there are practicalities. Sometimes deadlines fall at awkward times, bills need to be paid during the winter just as much as the Summer, and I am not someone who is comfortable shifting client sessions around if my bleed arrives two days late or early. And while the practicalities of this will differ from person to person and situation, there will be time for all of us when life must continue, however our energies are being pulled. This is not about creating any hard and fast rules for anyone or anything, but about providing frameworks for ourselves to adapt and flow with whatever life brings our way.

When I first began to learn about cyclical living, that frustrated me no end. Lisa Lister's fantastic book *Code Red* had attuned me to the "superpowers" of each phase of my menstrual cycle and I worried that if I didn't somehow lean into my energetic urgings and make the most of those each month, then I would have failed.

I hadn't gone on a date during the first half of my cycle when I was feeling most flirty and desirable? Or had been too busy to rest during my bleed time? Then somehow I felt I had missed my chance and was left feeling a little bereft... Until I realised that FOMO of that kind is another curse of a linear focus which becomes completely irrelevant in a cyclical life.

Because with no "beginning" or "end" we can never truly miss our shot at anything at all (imagine how much stress that might have saved Alexander Hamilton after all his talk about throwing away his shot? But I digress!) because what is meant to head our way will always come around again.

One of the first decks of oracle cards I bought was Goddess themed and included the Yoruba Goddess, Yemoja. Although it's not a deck I use now, the words associated with that card have stuck with me ever since, speaking of how we can never truly miss an opportunity because – just like the tides – everything that leaves us will always have the chance to wash back in.

At around the same time that deck came to me, I dreamed about my Nanna who had passed away a few years previously. In the dream she showed me a symbol and told me: "This means patience and faith; it's the lesson you need to learn in this lifetime. So much so that you should get it tattooed." I woke up unable to draw the symbol but with a clear picture of it in my mind so headed to Google images, where I found a Japanese Kanji identical to what I had just seen alongside the meaning, "To wait with certainty and allow your faith to carry you along."

In many ways, this is an important part of stepping out of the life and death duality; having the faith to wait patiently and faithfully rather than trying to control and force things to happen on our timescale. But isn't there a beauty in that? A beauty that allows us not only to be surprised by what might happen as we move between those points of life and death, but as we move outside of them too? A beauty that allows us to stay open to the possibility of rebirth that can only be found when we allow ourselves to embrace the experience of relinquishing something as a part of life, rather than the end of it.

Cyclical living

To live cyclically is to recognise that life was never meant to be a simple A to B and to recognise and embrace every part of what lies between and around those two points.

It is about ebbing, flowing and moving around to your inner rhythms in all ways and those of the outside world as they affect you, because there are many ways that can happen.

This topic could easily fill a whole book – and has. So many books have been written already about the cycles that affect us; about astrology and how our lives are influenced by the movements of the planets, about the Pagan wheel of the year and how the journey through the seasons impacts upon our energies and emotions, and about the menstrual cycles and those of the Moon and how tuning into either or both can support our journey through life. And if that simple paragraph says anything, then it's just how many different influences there are upon our energies at any given time.

It sounds complex – and it can well be, but it is also incredibly simple and completely natural to tune into the flow of energies within and around you and allow yourself – as far as possible – to live in line with those. At the end of this book you will find a wheel outlining roughly the many cycles that I personally try to honour within my life, and how those fit with the different energies we've discussed elsewhere within this book. One thing you'll notice is that for all of the many levels in that wheel, it all ties together incredibly neatly; in a way that almost invites us to live in and honour a constant state of flow.

Doing that will look different to each of us, because we are all unique. During my early forays into cyclical living, I felt like I must be doing something "wrong" if I didn't feel the ways the books and courses suggested I would during each week of the month; such was my disconnection from myself. Now I understand it wasn't my body or feelings that were wrong, but the idea we have all had drummed into us that there is one finite way to be and feel with which we will all naturally align.

No. That is precisely the opposite of what this is about.

Whatever the cycle or cycles you are paying attention to, living in accordance with those cycles for your own benefit takes trust and the kind of connection that is built by turning inwards and returning to what we find there time and time again, until eventually we learn to understand the language that comes from within. It takes discernment too; the ability to sit back and figure out our true energetic needs and pulls in comparison to those that come from someone or something else – like the times my body needs rest in comparison to those when she really wants me to move, but I'm feeling grumpy and would much rather zone out with Netflix.

As you've no doubt already guessed from the rest of this book, cyclical living means that we embrace it all; the dark and the light, the stop and the go. It means recognising that those places, and all of the many faceted flows between them are the most normal states in the world. And when every other part of the natural world moves in and through such phases of ebb and flow, how could we have ever thought ourselves to be any different?

But it hasn't always been that way. Here in the UK, many of our annual calendar dates are based around the agricultural year, with school and public holidays still based around the pre-industrial revolution days when so many people worked the land. There are often calls for those dates to change; shouts that individual weeks off in May and October respectively are outdated and could be moved to better fit with modern life. But those are calls you will rarely hear from me; largely because I love the way our calendar – even centuries after Romans, Vikings and others invaded these lands and imposed their structures and belief systems upon its inhabitants – very much align with the old wheel of the year my ancestors would have honoured. The wheel I still honour today.

The wheel of the year tells the story of nature through eight holy days or Sabbats, all of which can be found on the wheel at the end of the book. Today it's often associated with Paganism, since colonialism has long destroyed evidence of exactly what festivals the people who once honoured these lands celebrated. But with four of those days based specifically on the movements of the Sun, and the others tied intrinsically to changes in the seasons and the ways that would be reflected on the land, it seems to me that these are likely pretty close to those original festivals.

And let's not forget that for all our imbalanced societies and patriarchal religions have tried to wipe out so many of the old ways of thinking and being, some of those ways refused to go quietly. Undoubtedly this is why almost all of the Sabbats or festivals were co-opted by others who sought to harness their power either energetically – after all, rituals performed on those days tend to be supercharged – or simply by encouraging the locals to join in with their Christian practices without wholly betraying that which they held sacred.

Names of these festivals – and in some cases the overall calendar of festivals celebrated – differ from culture to culture, but it is no surprise that All Hallow's Eve falls on the same night as the festival of Samhain; that the return of the light at Yule is four days before Christmas; that the fertility and fire festival of Imbolc is also celebrated as Candlemass and that Ostara tends to fall so close to Easter, for starters. There are others that have no church equivalent – Beltane on 1st May and Lughnasadh on 1st August for example, but it is no coincidence that here in the UK the we continue to have public holidays in both of those months. And it's not just the dates themselves. Even today we carry forward traditions around those festivals, such as bringing an evergreen into the house in December to remind us that the darkness that precedes Yule won't last forever; and dancing around a Maypole – a fertility symbol, if ever I saw one – in quaint British villages during the fertility festival of Beltane. While the reasons for those traditions may have been lost in time, those actions and so many others are all grounded in the days when we honoured and worshipped nature and her cycles above all else.

The Eleventh Key: WILDNESS

Wildness is another idea that has become somewhat clichéd over recent years but as with so much of that, it's because it is bloody important. And is also as old as humanity – arguably even older.

To move outside of the duality of life and death and into a place of living cyclically is to reclaim a piece of our own wildness. It is to step outside of the demands of our societies to work on their timetable and to break away from this needless strain of constantly trying to control all of the energies around us and instead remember how to be *with* them.

Clarissa Pinkola Estés' classic book *Women Who Run with the Wolves* and Sharon Blackie's fabulous *If Women Rose Rooted* are both brilliant works on this topic, sharing the old myths of cultures that existed long before ours and reminding us of the power that can be found in the many aspects of our wildness.

One of my favourite myths which appears in both of those books is the tale of the selkie. It tells of a family of sister selkies; creatures who lived as seals for most of the month but, every Full Moon, would shed their skins and dance as beautiful women on the shores. On one occasion these women were spotted by a fisherman who fell in love and stole one of those skins, leaving the woman unable to transform back into her seal form. He asked her to stay on the shore and marry him – spending seven years with her after which he promised to return the skin.

The woman stayed and gave birth to a daughter whom she adored, but over time she began to fade – physically, emotionally and energetically, until she wondered if she could ever go on. After seven years she went to her husband and requested her skin, but he only laughed – why would he relinquish such a beautiful wife after all? But as the selkie's daughter grew, she understood her mother's need to be free and recognised that if her mother did not return to the sea, she would surely die. And so she dug into her father's possessions to retrieve the skin, handing it back to her mother, only for them to realise that the skin no longer fit, and faded away as she held it.

The selkie had almost given up hope and faded even further, but her daughter refused to accept that, and sent her away on a quest to meet a wise old woman tucked high in the hills, who told her how to find a new skin. And so she set off on that journey, finally coming across the skins of her sisters, killed and skinned by hunters since she had left them all. She grieved of course, but then – as instructed by the old woman – carried out a ritual that brought all but one of her sisters back to life as the seals they had always been, allowing them to slip into their skins and grieve their lost sister before heading back to the water and encouraging the woman to follow them. And so she would, but first she tucked the remaining skin into her own coat and went to her daughter, explaining the story and vowing to return every year throughout her life. While the daughter was sad and mourned, she understood that this was something her mother was unable to resist, and that this wildness was needed for her mother to not only survive, but to be fulfilled and in her wholeness… A wildness she too could experience, if ever she felt called to set off on a quest of her own.

Maybe part of the reason I love this story is the way it brings back my childhood dreams of being a mermaid. But I also love the story it tells of wildness as not just an urge, a call, but a need that lives within us, rooted in the truth of who we have always been. Not all of us will be called to venture to high in the hills or to change our skins forever; and nor will we need to leave our families behind and take to the seas forever.

But the journey back to wildness from our own places of entrapment may well require some sacrifice and change. It asks us to listen to the callings that speak so loudly from within us that they cannot be ignored; and to act upon them even when that action is scary and arduous. Because – as the story and those inner callings of ours remind us – scary and arduous is a small price to pay for the fulfilment that comes from living as the whole and wild version of ourselves.

EXERCISES AND PROMPTS

MEDITATION

Meet the archetypes of the seasons: Those four phases of the cycle of life and nature each have their own gifts to bring us. Use this journey to connect with the archetypes of those phases and embrace their gifts within yourself and your life.

RITUAL

Death ritual: We can all benefit from releasing what no longer serves us. This ritual, best carried out during the final days of the lunar cycle, will support you in doing just that – releasing and paying your respects to all that you no longer need.

Rebirthing ritual: Of course in the ever-turning cycle of life, rebirth always follows death. This ritual is perfect for the early days of a new lunar cycle – especially in the Spring – and invites you to rebirth a new version of yourself.

EXERCISES

- Take the time to track your physical feelings, emotions, strengths and challenges throughout the month in line with your own menstrual cycle and/or the cycles of the Moon, numbering those days starting from the first day of the New Moon or of your menstrual bleed, if appropriate.

After three or four months compare the notes you've taken and see where there are similarities from month to month.

- Create a timeline of all of the big and important events that have happened throughout your life, grouping them by month and by year. Once it is complete as far as feels right to you sit back and consider this all together; are there any repeated dates that are important for different reasons across the years? Are there any periods of the year that are particularly potent or important for you?

JOURNAL PROMPTS

- What do you need right now? Take the time to check in with yourself regularly. Journal on this from time to time – every day for a month or more, if that feels right to you.

- What are your beliefs around death?

- How would it be to see death as not an ending but an opportunity for rebirth?

- What if you were to relinquish control over life and surrender to the natural rhythms of your life and energy?

CREATIVITY

OUTCOME   POSSIBILITY

When I was 13, a moustached PE and Art teacher in too-short shorts, told my parents, "It's fair to say that Art isn't Ceryn's strong suit, but she does well elsewhere, so should probably concentrate on that." And right there, I learned the world would always appreciate me doing something well rather than something that was fun and – I thought – looked pretty.

Fast forward a few years to the time I shared my dreams of being a writer with a school careers advisor and was told I needed a "proper plan" – maybe I could use my writing in a practical way instead. Had I considered communications?

Of course, I'm not alone in my experiences. Because in cultures which tell us the arts aren't "valid" courses of study or work, cultures that perpetuate the tortured artist stereotype and focus heavily on the monetary value of everything, we are often told that anything remotely creative is only valid if we are objectively excellent at them and/or they will make us lots of money.

Let me say this loudly because it's important:

Creativity is about more than ticking boxes and making money. Creativity is about leaning into the possibilities that come when we stop trying to be perfect.

You might notice the word "be" cropped up in that sentence – something we've already talked about in this book. But in some ways the idea of balancing our being and our doing is never more potent than within the realm of creativity. Because isn't this so much of our problem, the fact that we are all educated to believe that creation of any sort is about the outcome; something that is in many ways the complete opposite of actual creativity?

In *Big Magic*, Elizabeth Gilbert talks about how, for the longest time, she didn't rely on her writing to pay the bills, simply because that put too much pressure on her creativity and often scared it away.

With that in mind, is it any wonder that so many of us find ourselves stuck – not only in terms of the pursuits we've been told are creative but also in terms of new ideas in other parts of our lives – after years of being told that everything we do is about the outcome; an outcome that must be "perfect"?

The perfect outcome

As my experiences at school, and the experiences many of us had both at school and for many years afterwards too, have all taught us one thing: that it's not the process that counts, only ever the end result. An end result which must always be objectively brilliant.

I don't know about you, but that's something I struggle with. Particularly after learning the hard way that the "perfect" outcomes on paper often felt nothing of the sort in many areas of my life.

This is probably why I find Danielle LaPorte's work on core desired feelings to be so damned powerful. In her book and course of that name, Danielle writes about the problems that can arise when we fixate on a particular outcome that we want to achieve or attain. Instead, she encourages us to focus on the ways we want to feel along that road; something I have always found so much more motivating with anything I've ever done.

Of course, when it comes to practical and logical tasks – the need to fulfil a specific goal, solve a particular problem or check a series of boxes – that is a relatively easy thing to achieve. But that's not the case with everything we do, and maybe this is exactly why those activities we call creative are considered to be so worthless in our society. In a world that has come to value practicality over joy, fun, and beauty, it's rare you will find a piece of art that is universally loved and lauded – meaning the results of those activities are generally considered to be useless.

Ridiculous isn't it? Particularly given how many of us find so much benefit in the arts. But of course they're not alone; consider just how many other important and beneficial jobs there are out there that are deemed to be useless, dull or menial, simply because the end result of them isn't universally adored.

I used to work with a woman who was excellent at creating interesting, exciting, even award-winning communications campaigns for staff at the company we worked for, which always brought about positive results in terms of the number of people who would take the actions she was trying to drive. When it came to the very practical side of communications she was brilliant. Yet when it came to sharing those ideas, she inevitably found herself lost; regularly asking for help from our colleagues on the wording to use and design concepts to brief into the marketing team while crying, "I'm just not creative!" It wasn't at all true of course. Her lack of confidence had nothing at all to do with her ability and everything to do with the fact that she didn't want to receive criticism on something she was unable to get tangibly "right."

And no wonder. As with so much of what we do, everyone likes to share their feedback; often with the best of intentions and, in the case of our jobs at least, usually because they have a vested interest in how something goes. But depending on the relationship we have with feedback, and on our own sense of rootedness within ourselves to stay centred no matter what is thrown our way, that can be damned difficult. It puts so much pressure on us to get a task "right" first time and find that place of perfection when there is almost never any such thing. It's a pressure that makes any task tougher.

After all, have you ever tried to be inspired on command? To relax into a place of imagination on a deadline? To truly do anything from a place of heart and soul when you know that thing will be completely torn apart afterwards? If not, let me tell you first-hand that it is bloody exhausting.

If you have never seen the Dr Who episode where the Doctor takes Vincent van Gogh to a modern exhibition of his work then I urge you to stop reading for a moment and check out the clip on YouTube right now. It never fails to make me cry.

By its very nature, creativity is about seeking, conceiving, gestating and birthing something new. And from the first moment a spark of inspiration is conceived, the world as you know it becomes different to the one everyone else sees because it is suddenly illuminated by a spark no-one else has seen, never mind comprehended. It never fails to send me into floods of tears at the way the world treated such great talent during his lifetime, only to hail him a genius long after he was around to hear it; at the fact that a person whose work is now adored by millions across the world, lived his entire life believing that he wasn't good enough at what he loved.

It's a belief that has plagued so many of us in so many ways for so long because we have been coached to believe that "good enough" means perfect, a concept that we humans were never meant to embody. A concept that, objectively speaking, is barely even real. So what if we were to take the feedback with a pinch of salt and instead of striving for what is "perfect," allow ourselves to be led a little further by the mystery of inspiration?

In many ways, creativity is one of the most archetypally lunar energies we can embody in the world. It speaks of growing something from nothing, holding that something within us and then releasing that out into the world when that something is ready to be born. But that is a key aspect of this – when it is ready. Because we often cannot control the outputs of what we create. Any attempt to force our creations into a certain place or form will only ever limit them – and us – into a place of less than we are capable of.

And when that certain place we are aiming for is a universally liked idea of perfection? Well then that limitation becomes even tougher because it removes all opportunity for learning, for growth, for evolution. It removes all possibility of what could be found along the way.

Embracing possibility

Creativity is not hard. It's one of the most natural things for, well, pretty much all of our Universe. I'm not just talking about creating life, although of course that happens a lot too, but instead about change, adaption and all things new.

We see creativity at work in the ways plants make themselves look and smell more irresistible to pollinators than their neighbours, and the way wild animals change and diversify over time specifically to hide from their predators.

I've seen it recently in the way Kali learned to navigate a temporary lack of sofa at home and found another way to jump up and bark at our mailperson out of the window. And in the way my favourite baby may not be quite ready to walk or crawl, but has learned to scoot anywhere he needs to go on his butt. And in the year prior to writing this we have all seen creativity at play in new businesses and other initiatives that have sprung up to support people through, and after, the Covid pandemic.

Creativity is inspiration; the moment when the spark of something arrives within you and needs to be heard, listened to and acted upon. It is the hope and liberation that comes when you suddenly see a way around something you've known for a long while wasn't right. But to embrace and even use those sparks, we must be open to a sense of possibility.

My friend, the artist and writer Gizem Evcin, would tell you that the muses of inspiration are always whispering to us. Our challenge is to listen to them – to step out of a world that is focussed wholly on logic, results and action and instead acquaint ourselves with the imaginal realms, where nothing at all is certain and absolutely everything is possible.

And it is this possibility that we have lost so much of, in our focus on playing it safe, logical and practical at every step. After all, how can we ever embrace the possibility of the new when we have been so deeply conditioned into the way things have always been?

By its very nature, creativity is fearless – a bit like the Fool in the tarot deck who is so entranced by possibility and new beginnings that they might just unwittingly step off a cliff and fall. Or, to paraphrase that famous line from Instagram accounts everywhere, they might just fly.

The terror of not knowing which it will be is a real thing, there's no doubt about it. But, as with so much of this work to reconnect and rebalance, the more we start to listen to our creativity, the more we come to know when it should be paused or put on a time out, and when it should be listened to and followed into the wilderness.

There is a wildness in creativity which invites us outside the box of everything we know and have been told, and instead offers the possibility of something new that hasn't been tried yet and is asking to be made real. Maybe it's a sign of how much we distrust the wild and the new that we are often taught to "harness our creativity" as though it's something we can tame and train to perform for us on our schedule and terms.

To an extent, of course that's true. Many of those who operate full time in the creative and imaginal realms will tell you about the daily rituals they employ to get in the zone; the schedules they arrange so they are working with rather than against their creative flow.

Yet sometimes I wonder what would happen if, just for a while, we allowed creativity to harness us instead?

What if we were to let it lead us into the wild for a short period of time, keeping our wits and footing about us as we went, but seeing where and how this energy would take us, where we'd end up and what our journey would be along the way?

In many ways, it's what I've done with this book. It began life back in 2018, when I completed the draft to a tight schedule and came up with something I was super proud of. A few months later I re-read the draft and realised it had no heart, soul and very little me. When it went off to an editor she advised similar and suggested the best thing would be to re-write it completely. And so I tried. Over and over again.

I tried to collate and make sense of the notes I'd taken, the linear thread of thought I was determined to follow; and got nowhere. Then one day, close to giving up, I grabbed a pen and an A4 notebook and declared out loud, "fine, let's do it your way then!" And here we are. One sore hand and a lot of – recycled – paper later, the first draft was created, completely different to my plans and expectations but something that feels so much more right. And here's the interesting thing about having allowed my creativity to run more wild than usual – that it gave me more than a book.

As I write this chapter, I have another notebook next to me full of ideas for a course, the beginnings of an entirely new book, and the missing pieces of an idea that has been hovering in the back of my mind for years. Of course, the trick was in befriending my creativity just enough to stay close, rather than run away with all those other ideas in the meantime. But maybe there was also a trick in teaching my logical, outcome-driven brain to step back too and allow the odd meander into the wilderness without getting frustrated that I wasn't staying wholly on track.

Of course there must be a balance if we can. After all, we've all heard tales of the tortured artists who found themselves so tightly tethered to the wild nature of creativity that they struggled to exist in the outside world. Earlier I wrote about Van Gogh's ability to see the world differently to those around him, but in truth that's only half the story – he *lived in a* different world to those around him. And no matter what the rest of the world may have told him was "real," he knew better. He saw in the broader spectrum of colour and light; he knew the wildness his creativity was calling him to so well, that once he had ventured there, he struggled to return.

In many ways, creativity – while so often rooted somehow in our physical reality – will always spend most of its time in a place that is anything but physically "real" – of course it will. According to the NHS, psychosis is defined as, "When people lose some contact with reality. This might involve seeing or hearing things that other people cannot see or hear (hallucinations) and believing things that are not actually true (delusions)." There are many dimensions to psychosis which are terrifying and dangerous for the person having those experiences, but such a broad definition could also be applied to many other circumstances, including a person in the throes of creativity. My wise friend, L Harris, writes incredibly insightful and powerful pieces on the subject of psychiatric oppression, and writes so potently of the need for people who don't conform to the norms of our world to put on a performance; as well as the ways in which words like "normal" represent yet another binary that can be both limiting and dangerous.

By telling us what is and isn't "normal", the world says it's trying to keep us safe – and given how terrifying a psychotic episode can be, there's potentially something in that. But the strict parameters of that "normality" can also keep us from truly allowing ourselves to step into the wildness of creativity; from taking us out of the pursuit of an outcome we are led to believe life must always be, and instead giving us a safe space to dance with the possibilities offered by the wild.

The joy of true creativity

To be in a state of creativity is to be in flow with those imaginal realms, but equally to be in flow with the whole of this natural world.

We so often speak of mindfulness as the practice of being in the present – and that's true. But we must also remember the creative power held in the present moment that is so challenging to be in contact with, if our attention is placed anywhere else in time.

When we're stuck regretting the past, we are looking at something that can't be changed, that has already been created.

When we're pulled anxiously into worries of the future, our minds are already concocting definitive results based only on what we know to be true right now.

But it doesn't have to be that way. In many ways the past and the future offer such fuel for inspiration, if we can allow ourselves to flow with, rather than get stuck in them. A wandering mind can be the place that reminds us of the passions that drive us and the past challenges we're determined to help others through. It can be the thing that allows us to dream about a world in which things could be different, in which maybe new possibilities can be enjoyed and made use of.

Of course, we must come back to the here and now to use those inspirations and reach whatever outcome they will lead towards. But we must also encourage our creativity – that expansive part of ourselves – to venture to the times and places we tell the more logical parts of our mind they can't be trusted with.

Maybe this is why our culture has become so wedded to the idea that creativity = the arts, because the outputs from those fields often live so clearly outside of logic and objectivity.

That's not to say the more artful side of life isn't important though, gods no. Just look at the way we all talk about movies, tv shows and music; the way a single song has the power to change the mood of a whole day and whisk you back to a memory as though you were physically there. And look at the way two dimensional images on a wall can inspire so much joy and wonder within us. Art is important, powerful and much more than our output-driven culture would have us believe. But it is also not the limit of our creativity; and in being educated away from everything it encompasses, in our drive for functionality and objectivity, we are not only missing out on the beauty of art, but are creating even broader problems for each and every one of us.

How do we overcome the challenges we face as a planet if we can't think creatively enough to change the ways things are done?

How do we change our imbalanced, restrictive systems of power if we are unable to think outside of the boxes that we've grown up with and learned?

And how do we solve the myriad of mental health problems we as a species are experiencing if we don't give ourselves the freedom to embrace the flow?

How many world-changing scientific discoveries have come from someone stepping outside of the box of certainty and embracing their creativity long enough to ask what if? And how many other every day sparks of inspiration and curiosity – from milking a cow, to kicking a ball around a field, and rubbing two sticks together to create fire – have so deeply altered the world we live in and lives we lead?

We see the results of creativity at play in every facet of our lives. So why are we so often discouraged from embracing the one thing that could lead us to change?

I sometimes wonder if that is precisely why. After all, we all know the upsets that come in some parts of society when we suggest that change is needed, never mind the fear that undoubtedly arises when we allow ourselves to get curious about the possibilities to get creative and do things differently. For all the good it would do – alongside some bad of course, not every spark of inspiration comes with the best of intentions or ends up being implemented as such. Creativity also has the potential to seriously affect the order of things we've so often been told is "natural."

Creativity can be found and honoured in any and every part of our lives and our world, and it can benefit both. Like so many of the things in this book, it simply requires us to stop living inside the fear of failure and imperfection we have been conditioned into and instead, as Rachel Rodgers writes in her book *We Should All Be Millionaires,* ask, "What would I do if I weren't being good?" But for that to happen we must also step away from the idea that we "can't," that all of the best ideas are taken, and that we are somehow exempt from the utterly natural energy of creation which led us and everything we see and know into being.

When we do that, when we remember our place as part of that creative energy, then instead we can spread our wings not to fall, but to leap into the slipstream of its flow.

The Twelfth Key: BEAUTY

When it comes to the key to re-balancing this area of our lives, there are many we could use; from becoming re-enchanted by life until that enchantment carries us away into somewhere new, to re-connecting with the need to play in our lives so that we can embrace that sense of possibility, rather than focus on the outcomes.

But as I wrote this chapter, the word I returned to time and time again was beauty, and to the concept of embracing true beauty within our lives.

If that word makes you shudder, I understand why. The very idea of beauty has been weaponised against us and defined as an ever-changing standard we must force ourselves to live up to, in order to be considered "enough," no matter the cost or energy that takes. But the beauty I am referring to is not some scale leading up to perfection that requires nips, tucks or air brushing to achieve. Hell, it's not even related to physical attractiveness, and to limit beauty in such a way – to limit ourselves like this is frustrating at best and downright abusive at worst; bullshit designed to tell us who should and shouldn't be heard, seen and even respected.

That's not to say that doing what you want to look a certain way is a problem; there is nothing at all wrong in nourishing and accentuating yourself in ways that feel joyful, fun and pleasurable to you. It's when we feel that we *must* do those things to be deemed worthy, that this becomes a problem.

Real, true beauty is nothing like that and is so much easier to reach. It's what comes when we step back and allow ourselves to embrace life fully, a place where so often we cannot help to be inspired.

Beauty is a feeling of connection to something so glorious that it takes our breath away. It is that moment we witness something so heart-breakingly lovely that it warms our hearts and brings tears of pure emotion to our eyes in even the darkest of moments; and is the thing that leaves its impression, not only on your eyes or libido but on your heart and your senses, long after your interaction with it is done.

Let me share some of the most beautiful things I've ever witnessed:

The moment I stood by a lake in my favourite place on Earth just as the Sun broke through the grey clouds of a shower and was momentarily blown away by the way everything came together so perfectly – the colours, the light, the peace and the contentment – to create a feeling of pure oneness with the world and a sense of utter love for it.

Watching Fleetwood Mac play *The Chain* live at Wembley Stadium and feeling the baseline cut through the still, warm summer air and go straight into my nervous system, until it buzzed through every part of my body and felt like it ignited my soul.

The time my lovely brother came home late from work because he'd stumbled across an old man who'd fallen on the pavement and not only called an ambulance and the man's daughter, but also stayed with him throughout the whole experience even after a long day at work, asking questions and telling jokes until he and his daughter headed off in the ambulance.

I wonder sometimes what the difference is between love and beauty. In many ways, the two feel similar when I tune in and experience them – like a oneness or transcendence that puts me into a flow of gratitude at this incredible world I'm a part of, the Universe I belong to and the life I get to live. And maybe the truth is that the two go hand in hand; that love is the fullness which inevitably comes when we allow ourselves to align with and embrace beauty.

The world has told us that those are things we must look for outside of ourselves – that we cannot be "complete" without them. But all that has ever served to do is cut us off from the feeling of glorious expansion that comes when we stop looking for things that will "make us" beautiful and instead allow ourselves to be filled with beauty – our own and that of this whole glorious planet.

How do we do that? We allow ourselves to surrender to it.

We take off the eyes of tiredness and frustration, through which we so often see the world around us, and instead allow ourselves to be enchanted by the wonder that explodes from this place we call home and comes when we see it with fresh, childlike eyes.

We let ourselves play – in any way that feels right to us – as a child would play, not in a way that strives towards an outcome of any sort, but just in a way that feels enjoyable and allows us to express ourselves in whatever way we want and need to.

We step out of the mundane and the everyday and take ourselves on an adventure – whether that be a trip overseas or a different route to the local shop – simply to see what we find there.

We immerse ourselves in the sensual pleasures of good food, sex, dancing and more with no agenda other than to allow ourselves to feel good.

And we take in the art which is so often aligned with creativity; be it in a cinema, a gallery, a concert venue or from the comfort of our own home and allow ourselves to be truly immersed in those things.

None of this is with the intention of escaping reality, but with embracing it. Of truly surrendering to the moments as they come, to the experiences as we go through them and to the emotions as they rise and fall, knowing that the force behind each of those things is the true fuel that drives us forwards.

To do this is to align ourselves with all of those energies and remember that, regardless of what anyone else may say or think they, and we, are filled with beauty.

EXERCISES AND PROMPTS

MEDITATION

Meet your muse: That creative force is something we can all connect to and work with. So join me on a journey to meet your own muse – the personification of that work who will support your own creativity.

RITUAL

Align yourself with beauty: In this ritual we will work to align ourselves more fully with the true energy of beauty. This one will work extra well if conducted outdoors where you can fully embrace the beauty of nature!

EXERCISES

- Take the time to create something – anything. What you create or how it looks, sounds, feels or tastes when you're done is irrelevant. Just allow yourself to be in that place of creation.

- Equally allow yourself to play. Whether it be hopscotch in the street, board games with your loved ones, joining in with your favourite little people's imaginary play or something else entirely, just take the time to return to that childish part of you who so enjoyed the space to play.

- Thinking about what you would like to bring into your life, create a vision board – but make sure the images and words you use here aren't just of the specific outcomes you want to create. Consider the broader ways that will impact your life, how you intend to feel and why this is important to you.

JOURNAL PROMPTS

- What is your relationship with feedback?

- What do you avoid or hold back on for fear of not being perfect?

- What were your favourite games as a child?

- What does the word beautiful mean to you?

- What do you do simply because you enjoy it?

- What are your most beautiful experiences?

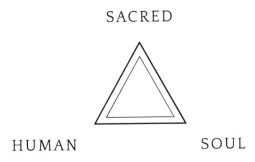

SACRED

HUMAN   SOUL

One of my greatest pet peeves in the circles I've often moved within, is the idea that to be human is somehow a failure; that our "human" selves are somehow less than our spiritual.

You know what I mean here, the eye rolls when someone asks what a chakra is; the bemoaning of those days that, "I'm just being so very human, sigh;" and perhaps worst of all, the declarations that, "I'm just so spiritual!"

I get it, I really do. I have been – and continue to go – through my own process of spiritual awakenings and soul integrations and know there are points in those cycles where even the most grounded of us will do an internal eye roll at those who just don't get it.

But those are the parts we move through quickly; parts we must move through quickly, if we are ever to reach a point of integration and move forward from a more soulful perspective. Because while the human and the soulful are very much just different sides of the same coin, the soulful and the arrogant? They're very different ends of a pretty wide spectrum.

And while our human and soul selves definitely have some very different characteristics, including the limitations that each is bound by, to suggest that either is any less sacred or powerful than the other doesn't just diminish that single part of us, but the whole of ourselves and the soulfully human lives they could be living.

Being human

When I speak about our human selves, I refer to the you that walks, talks and feels in the here and now. Our human selves are considered by some to be "less than" our souls thanks to their needs for things like food and water and their obedience to the laws of time and space; not to mention the fact that they can be so easily distracted or impacted by emotions. And those human parts of us can be beholden to fear, that's true, but only because there is a lot that can damage them.

That fear is much of the reason why life can feel so much harder when we focus solely on our human selves and entirely bypassing our souls. By that I mean living a life of what Mariana Caplan calls ego separation in her book *Eyes Wide Open*; the over-reliance on "I" and "me" that so many of us experience when we focus too heavily on our human selves. This leads us to believe we are separate from everyone and everything else in the world, rather than seeing ourselves as part of the whole. And there are other pitfalls too: getting so caught up in the day to day that we rarely step back to consider anything bigger. Then we lose ourselves in the frustration that can come, when we truly believe we are only as powerful and as wise as the day to day will allow. And allowing that frustration and the fear that sits behind it to limit us from the possibilities of change, beauty and new-ness that are always available to us, no matter how stuck we may have been feeling.

Maybe it is the perceived stuckness and limitations which is why our human self is often conflated with other parts of us that can feel negative, like the ego voice that tries so hard to protect us, or the shoulds and must nots that have been drummed into us by society. But while it's true that both of those voices connect only to our human selves, they are not in themselves our human-ness. No, our human-ness is much more expansive than that.

And even the limitations we experience within this aspect of ourselves were never intended to diminish it. But were and are a crucial part of the very reason we are here:

To experience life on Earth.

It is our human selves that feel, and while that runs the risk of heartbreak and anguish, it also provides us with the opportunity for true excitement, utter joy and real hilarity.

It is our human selves that get to enjoy the physical...no, your soul can't taste an amazing piece of cake, feel the sand beneath its toes or have a mind-blowing orgasm – only the memory of those things.

And equally, it's your humanity that takes the action, drives the change and experiences this Earth for more than it is.

It's true that the physical and emotional aspects of our humanity can feel restrictive from time to time of course. Those times we're deeply inspired in a project but need to break to sleep, eat or exercise, or those when something utterly awful happens that sends our emotions to rock bottom for days on end. But to see those things wholly as restrictions, denies so much of the power they offer us. A power that grounds us back into the here and now during the times that inspiration and creativity would drag us out into the wilderness never to be seen again; and a power that reminds us of exactly why change is so important to us and pushes us to move forwards even when hope seems to wane.

When we diminish our human selves and try to pass them off as being some sort of burdensome sidekick, our superhuman souls are forced to drag through life. We ignore so much of what they have to offer us and so much of the power that being human involves.

Meggan Watterson often uses the line, "Your body is your soul's chance to be here," and this is exactly it.

Your human self is the one who gets to be here, in all of its perfect imperfection, to carry out its mission for this life and beyond and to leave the kind of legacy – big or small – that makes a difference not only in your lifetime or even in the lives of all those that will follow, but for this Earth. What could be more beautiful, powerful and important?

Getting soulful

Trying to define the soul is where things start to get a bit more complicated. We can all agree on what it is to be human, since our human-ness cannot be easily ignored or denied. The spiritual or soulful part though? That's a bit more complex, simply because every school of thought and belief – in some ways every person within each of those schools – has its own views and ideas.

There are many who will tell you that we are what we see in the mirror every day and that's it. In case you hadn't already guessed, I am not one of those people, and of course, what I've written here is based predominantly on my own views, beliefs and experiences.

To me, the soulful and spiritual parts of us are the bits that are eternal, wise and unlimited. They are the parts that see and know so much more than our human eyes and minds allow, but that so often take a backseat in the everyday because that's what they agreed when we decided to come to Earth for this as a human. In order to gain the benefit of our own souls, we must take the time to connect to them, trust them – things that are not tangible and that no-one else can (so far) actually provide tangible proof of.

This intangible part of us goes by different names, and it's easy to think that they are interchangeable. Some are, but I'm of the belief that there are different aspects of the Divine part of us, specifically the spirit and the soul as outlined in Bill Plotkin's *Soulcraft*. In that book, he uses a definition of soul that I will refer to here in using that term, which is: "The vital, mysterious and wild core of our individual selves, an essence unique to each person, qualities found in layers of the self, much greater than our personalities," while defining spirit as, "The single, great and eternal mystery that permeates and animates everything in the universe and yet transcends it all."

I often think of our soul selves as our extra consciousness; the part that exists outside of our lived and, in many ways, logical experience but is still very much a unique part of our essence. It also has access to a broader bank of collective wisdom and insights than those we consciously recognise, a bank that can be found to belong to something broader and greater than any or all of us which Bill would call spirit.

You will often hear people talk about their Higher Selves – the part of them that is most aligned with the Divine. But while that makes a lot of sense, it can also be deceptive; because to align "higher" with "more spiritual" is to miss something vital within us. It misses the importance of rooting down into the Earth, our ancestry, our shadows and the depths of all that is available to us – something that this witch can say from experience is a critical part of bringing the wisdom and power of our soul into the everyday.

Whatever its name, this part of us can bring so many blessings. I can't tell you how many clients I have worked with over the years who have felt completely stuck with a particular behavioural pattern or relationship until they've had access to the ways in which those patterns are replaying matters from outside of their current life, patterns that can either be found in other lifetimes their souls have experienced or that have been carried forward within them from their ancestors.

And speaking personally, there are countless times that a connection to my soul – or to the wider, collective wisdom she has access to, has provided me with the kind of bigger picture insights that changed my whole perspective on something. The unerring side-by-side support that just isn't always possible from physical loved ones, or the clarity that is so easy to see when you've played this game called life goodness knows how many times before.

I wholly believe that embracing our souls within the everyday is something that can enrich and empower every part of our lives more times over than I can express. But there are challenges and pitfalls with this part of us too. Not least the fact that it is unable to take any of the actions that will support us to effect change, in our own lives or in the world around us. It can nudge and prepare us to do that, but it cannot take the steps without input from and support for its human counterpart.

A less tangible way of avoiding that action comes when we focus all of our attentions on our extra conscious selves to the point of what has come to be known as spiritual bypassing. That phrase is used a lot nowadays to describe the ways many people will "love and light" away things that are otherwise too painful or unpleasant to face, dismissing their own experiences and those of others along the way.

I know of a wonderful mother who lost her young daughter after years of physical health problems and was told in the days afterwards, "Don't be sad, everything happens for a reason." Insensitive much?!

I've also heard of more than a handful of people who choose not to take action on environmental issues because, "I do all of my planetary healing on the meditation mat;" and those who refuse to acknowledge social justice matters because, "Division is only an illusion" – easy to say when you're not personally experiencing the oppression that division brings. Then there is the story I once heard about a woman who believed she could comfortably spend her weekends in a haze of tequila cocktails and cocaine without worrying about the effects of either on her body because she ingested both with, "the highest intention."

No. To every one of those things, no. Because while you can absolutely believe in a bigger picture in which even the hardest of situations somehow make sense; while you can definitely meditate and pray for global healing and world equity; and while I'm in no way suggesting we all must live lives of sobriety; we are citizens of this planet, members of humanity, and custodians of these glorious human bodies which have so much to offer the world. Those are responsibilities we must take seriously. Otherwise what is the point in our wise and powerful souls even bothering to venture here?

But spiritual bypassing isn't the only pitfall of a wholly soul-focussed life. Heading back to the book *Eyes Wide Open*, Mariana Caplan includes a whole chapter dedicated to what she calls, "Spiritually transmitted diseases;" the pitfalls of getting too carried away with our spirit rather than grounding into ourselves. She lists 11 of these in total, from fast food spirituality (the weekend courses that promise enlightenment) to pseudo spirituality (dressing and talking like those who have undertaken lengthy periods of their own soul work, with the belief that makes us just like them). I'm embarrassed but not ashamed to say I've experienced almost all of the 11 at some point in time, as many of us on this path have. The difference comes when we choose not to stay in them and to come back to ourselves instead.

Perhaps the most dangerous of everything Mariana writes about is what she calls "the deadly virus;" the idea of having somehow arrived at a place of pure and utter enlightenment as though there is nowhere further to go. I've been moving in these Western spiritual circles for some years now and have seen people fall into this trap many times before. Hell, it's another of the traps I've fallen into myself on occasion.

Here's one rule for spotting those who are likely to be the safest and most grounded of teachers and guides: they're usually the ones who speak about spirituality, while also admitting they don't have every piece of their own shit together and who recognise that neither part of us is perfectly suited to life here on Earth by itself.; They are those who are gloriously, imperfectly, soulfully human

The sacred whole

In many ways, the work of a therapist is always to quieten the voices of separation that live within us and bring us back to a place of our own wholeness. But when I became a therapist, I realised I wanted to take that one step further and help people to re-member and integrate their own sacred wholeness.

For me, this reunion is what happens when we not only connect with our soul and the wonderfulness it offers, but also integrate that soul with the human parts of us and come to remember that both our human and our soul selves hold power, wisdom and beauty and can absolutely be considered sacred.

I know, that word is another that can trigger deep wounding in us. Sacred, soul and spirit are words we so often see through the eyes of religion and what we have been told to believe in. But in reality, what we're talking about here isn't linked to religion, or about any sort of spiritual belief system. Instead this is about finding meaning in life.

For those with a particular belief system, the two will inevitably come together with our meaning allowing us to feel somehow connected to whatever it is that we consider greater than ourselves; be that God, Goddess, Nature or the Marvel Comics, but that's not always the way.

Maybe your meaning is about making the world a better place and leaving a legacy of some sort behind you. Maybe it's about doing your bit in support of those causes that matter to you or against those things that boil your blood. Or maybe for you, meaning is simply about making the most of every day, about shining that light of yours out into the world and about taking care of those who matter most to you, in the hope that it will encourage others to do the same.

No-one else gets to tell you what that meaning is because it is a personal one that is so key to our own unique selves – both the soul and the human. Although other people can often identify the signposts that bring us back to our own sense of meaning, simply by the way some almost divine spark seems to ignite within us whenever we do and talk about them.

In truth though, we often don't need another person to tell us what brings meaning within our lives because that's the thing we already know seems to fill up every part of our being on even the toughest of days and inevitably leaves us feeling wholly and completely ourselves.

It's something our soul undoubtedly knows all too well, and will happily nudge us back to when we have forgotten. And something that our human selves will always feel invigorated to take part in. But most of all it's the thing that undoubtedly causes us to reunite those parts of ourselves even long before we consciously try.

Once we have identified those things, we can start to embrace them within ourselves in our lives in a way that pulls us out of the inertia we can so easily fall into, if we are drowning in the motions of the everyday or numbing the pain of what it is to be human. When we can do that, when we can allow meaning to take the wheel of our lives, that's when we can truly start to live a soulful life.

The Thirteenth Key: GROUNDING

I sometimes think that soul work – the task of integrating our human and soul selves – requires us to play the part of a lightning rod every single day.

We tap into the soul that we know is there, that we can feel around us but not always within us. And then find a way to draw it wholly into ourselves not just during moments on a meditation mat or while we stand and watch a glorious sunset, but in as many moments, hours, weeks and years as we can, until eventually we have integrated our soul into each and every facet of our lives.

That cannot happen, though, until we learn how to ground ourselves; into this Earth and human life, for all the practical and tangible benefits it can offer us and our purpose, but also into our selves. The selves that our souls are and have always been part of.

In many ways, this thirteenth key is where much of what we have spoken about in this book converges. It's where we break out of the ideas of separation that have been forced upon us and instead get to know ourselves for everything that we are and can be.

It's where we work through the knowledge, insight, power and beauty that comes from outside and within us and tune into all of the different voices of ourselves, as we allow them to lead us back to a place of our own centre.

Grounding comes when we allow our physical selves – and all of their needs – to be considered sacred exactly as they are, and we live our lives in accordance with that. It comes when we recognise ourselves not as single trees standing alone on the Earth but as one part of an incredible, interconnected forest of life.

Grounding is what happens when we shake off the shame that has been conditioned into us and recognise the Divinity within every part of ourselves. It is the vital ingredient that enables us to make the everyday sacred and the sacred every day.

EXERCISES AND PROMPTS

MEDITATION

Recognising your Divinely human self: Earlier we took a journey to meet your whole self, but what if we were to take this one step further? This journey invites you to meet the Divinely human version of yourself who perfectly blends both facets of that to bring you face-to-face with your greatest power and potential.

RITUAL

Embracing your human and Divine: Following on from the journey above, this ritual will support you in anchoring both your humanity and your soul fully within your everyday self.

EXERCISES

Take part in a physical activity that you enjoy; maybe a walk, dancing, sex, exercise or eating something delicious. Whatever it is, set the intention beforehand to make this a living, breathing embodiment of your soul and an act of gratitude to all that you hold sacred. Undertake this consciously, embracing every single sensation of it, as you allow yourself to be beautifully, soulfully human.

JOURNAL PROMPTS

- What are your feelings on being human?

- How do you perceive the idea of soul?

- What would it mean to you to be soulfully human?

- What inspires you?

- What do you want your legacy to be?

- What do you hold most sacred and meaningful?

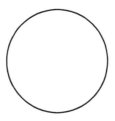

space

The place in between where all things are possible, yet nothing is set. The place of pure potential.

Space is the presence of all and the absence of any. The home of the mystery, the place of creation.

In Space we have no choice but to surrender, to hand over our dreams and allow source to take charge and we learn the whole of our power and the truth of the all.

We welcome Space in the Centre; in the time between times and the ever-turning wheel.

In Space, we embrace the unknown that lies beyond; that which can no longer be felt or seen or sensed.

We cannot know and we do not try.

We trust that with Space what has gone will return.

We trust that in Space only love can remain.

To be without Space is to hold tightly to a control we can never

And to restrict Space is to keep one in a life which is long past its best.

But to leave Space unbounded is to never find form; to float ceaselessly with no hope of rebirth.

But Space is the place of conception in which all can be made manifest. It is the long unseen place of our dreams and our power.

True Space is needed for the whole of our balance.

So we call to the Centre and to Space, to the Goddess and the God, to the Soul and the Mystery and to all that lies between.

We call to our helpers, our teachers our guides; to the galaxies and universes, to all that has been and is ever to be.

And we ask them to join with us, to work with us and to bless us with their protection, their possibility and their power. And together we complete our circle of sacred balance.

To the Centre, to Soul, to Spirit and the Space, hail and welcome.

So it is and it is so.

To hear this invocation in full, along with a short story, **The Old Woman Who Weaves the Universe,** visit the additional materials link at the back of the book.

CONCLUSION

Here's the part where you get to make a choice

My conscious journey to Divine Feminism began when I started tracking my cycles and re-membered that once that was the norm; that there was a time when the world worked for, rather than against us.

But in many ways it began years and years before that when I watched an episode of Buffy the Vampire Slayer – a show that had previously felt like such a feminist awakening for me – and heard how the first slayer was created when a teenage girl was imbued with the powers of a shadow demon in order to fight evil on behalf of a group of men. When Buffy heard that story she was furious at the abuse and oppression it involved. But honestly? I think I was more furious.

I remember wondering why this powerful lineage of women had to come from a demon – something the show had spent five years telling us was evil. And wanting nothing more than to see all of the slayers throughout time team up to defeat not only the demons and the vampires they were meant to fight, but also all of those who had ever suggested their power was something wrong, evil, negative.

Looking back, I recognise that triggered something in my soul; a memory of those who stepped into what was once a balanced and full world and chose not to embrace the beauty that involved, but to destroy it in pursuit of their own power. To destroy us, and to do what they could to break and diminish us time and time and time again.

We can give that force many names; patriarchy, the dark Annunaki, the sons of Belial, oppression or evil to name but a few. I've referred to patriarchy within this book because it is the one that seems most simple, but in truth there is another I refer to generally outside of the pages of a book or the recordings of a podcast: pathetic scumbags so insecure in their own power that they have devoted themselves to taking ours – so much of ours.

No more.

Because while I've seen so many of the ways their actions have impacted us and the world; so much of the pain and destruction they have caused, I've also seen the world that came before that too – a world I truly believe we can get back to.

Divine Feminism doesn't invite us to go back, only to go forwards; returning to the fundamental principles of connection, balance and flow that were and always will be the foundation of this planet. But this time equipped with everything we've learned and gained along the way.

In many ways, this book is a step-by-step invitation to reclaim those principles and everything that they involve for yourself and your own life. It invites you to quiet the voice of your own separation, to return to a place of wholeness, and of the synergy that can be found when we reconnect, not only inwardly but outwardly too – in a safe and supportive way that honours our own needs and those of the world around us.

If, even now, that sounds like a lot, then I understand. But remember this isn't about asking you to become anything new. It is simply a case of allowing ourselves to return to a state that is, quite simply, us.

The us we have always been and always were before we were told we were anything less and before we were forced to be anything different.

The journey to get there won't necessarily be easy. We are unpacking the conditioning of years, generations and lifetimes. And it will take a hefty dose of discernment to weed through all of the voices and urges that would try to keep us small.

The forces outside of us that have long taken root within us will fight back. We will fight harder. When our fears rise up, we will tackle them with hearts, souls, minds and bodies of fire, and with the self-belief that comes in knowing they only rise because they know they are about to be beaten.

But our fighting won't all take the forms they are used to, because we recognise that the true ways to reclaim our wholeness are through embracing all that they are so afraid of. The power that exists for all rather than for some. The beautiful wildness of life on this Earth and the glorious, shameless pleasure of what it is to be human.

This is a big journey, but one that we take hand in hand, side by side with so many others that have come before us and are yet to dance in the joys of sacred balance, as they walk this beautiful world from a place of flow and connection.

It is a big task, but one that we don't need to complete overnight. And if it starts to overwhelm you, just remember the words of my dad – a man who, while as much a member of our out-of-balance society as we all are, has never taught me that I am anything less than whole and powerful, no matter how much the outside world may have drowned out his voice: "How do you eat an elephant? One bite at a time."

"I hate this. I hate being here. I hate that you have to be here. I hate that there's evil and that I was chosen to fight it. I wish a whole lot of the time that I hadn't been. I know a lot of you wish I hadn't been, either.

This isn't about wishes.

This is about choices.

I believe we can beat this evil. Not when it comes. Not when its army is ready. Now. Tomorrow morning, I'm opening the seal. I'm going down into the Hellmouth and I am finishing this, once and for all. Right now, you're asking yourself what makes this different? What makes us anything more than a bunch of girls being picked off one by one? It's true. None of you have the power that Faith and I do.

So here's the part where you make a choice. What if you could have that power, now? In every generation, one Slayer is born, because a bunch of men who died thousands of years ago made up that rule. They were powerful men. This woman is more powerful than all of them combined.

So I say we change the rule.

I say my power, should be our power.

Tomorrow, this woman will use the essence of this scythe to change our destiny. From now on, every girl in the world who might be a Slayer, will be a Slayer. Every girl who could have the power, will have the power. Can stand up, will stand up. Slayers, every one of us.

Make your choice.

Are you ready to be strong?"

- Buffy the Vampire Slayer, Chosen (2003)

ACKNOWLEDGMENTS

There are so many people I want to thank for the parts they've played in the long and wild ride that has been the creation of this book.

First of all my incredible family, every last one of them – Rowntrees, Lavenders, Boldons, Currys, Fells, Gouchs, Leas, Schofields and Weatherspoons alike; and most especially my Mum, Dad (who doesn't, for the record, eat actual elephants) and Jamie for their eternal support and the foundation they've always given me from which to explore the world.

To Inka for the laughter and walk breaks, and to Kali for being the best familiar, roommate, writing coach, friend, cuddle provider and lockdown buddy a woman could ask for.

To the women of the She Power Coven, the midwives who held space for the first iteration of this book to be brought to life, and especially to my book witch Susan, wise one Leah, and intuitive queen Marci.

To the circle that grew from that space and the elemental witches that are the compass for me and my work: Rachael – the heart and sounding board for so much of this book, and the only woman I'll ever walk that damned labyrinth with, Sarah Beth, Shaina and Gizem. Thank you for knowing me, for supporting my healing journey and for bringing me back to myself and my wildness. And to Sean, Julian, Lin and Nathalie – thank you for holding my witches so they could hold me.

To Becca and Sarah for walks on the beach, to Dishy, Helen, Louise, Stacey and Liz for making me laugh and showing me a different perspective; to Emily for telling me when I was keeping myself small; to Kate, Amy, Kirsty, Ameara, Leanne, Emma and Nicola for believing in me even when I wavered; to Vicky, Dawn and Kathryn for always, always making me smile; and to Emily, Rachel, Sara and Caz for being the most kick ass feminists a woman could hope to know.

To the DNA activating superhero and author of this book's sister, Yolandi, for awakening my warrior priestess, and to Charlie and the Untamed Soul family for encouraging me to own my weird.

To the very first editors of this book Allison and Veronica – without the two of you the Divine Feminist would never have made it anywhere near print!

To Nicola and the Unbound Press family for holding this book baby of mine – and me – with such fierce, courageous tenderness and bringing us both out into the world.

To Leah Kent for the STUNNING book cover and design and to Becky Wright for the amazing photos!

To Damian, Keith, Andy, Alan and Ryan for proving to me that there are good men out there even when I was scared to look for them.

To the Connecting the Dots family for their Monday morning check ins, laughter and inspiration, and especially to Sarah for connecting the dots to make this book a reality.

To Maya, Meggan, Lisa, Rob, Carmel, David, Bethany and the teachers of the Alef Trust; Mark, Ian and the people of Reboot; and to all of the authors in the list overleaf; for your insights and for all I've learned from and because of you.

To Tai Morgan for the incredible Divine Feminist logo, and to Mama Moon candles, Lisa Serle of the Modern Witch Tarot, Billie Eilish for You Should See Me in a Crown, Josie Danielle for Light Language, Nicole Perkins and Bim Adewunmi for the Thirst Aid Kit podcast, and Chris Evans for, well, being Chris Evans – the muses that inspired this book into being.

To all of my wonderful clients over the past six years – from early days in a Northumberland village hall to 1:1 sessions and online communities; I won't name you all (confidentiality and all that!) but every single one of you has taught me something and I am richer for knowing you. Thank you. And for Julie especially, know a copy of this book with your name on it will always be close to my heart.

To my ancestors, guides and inspirers – all of you for the support, the wisdom and the love. And especially to Lilith; the patron of this book and of the Divine Feminist.

And finally to you for reading this. May you reconnect to yourself and return to a place of wholeness and flow that allows us to rebalance our own lives and the whole of this world!

ADDITIONAL MATERIALS

Additional materials for this book, including recordings of all meditations and elemental invocations, and instructions for each ritual can be found at **www.divinefeminist/book-resources**

You can also learn more about me and the Divine Feminist by following **@divine.feminist** on Instagram or checking out the podcast of the same name at **www.cerynrowntree.com/divinefeminist**

Meanwhile listen to the playlist on Spotify that inspired this book and continues to inspire so much of this work (all additional track suggestions welcome!) by scanning the code below or visiting the resources link above.

REFERENCES

Please visit **www.divinefeminist/book-resources**
for a list of recommended reading.

Chimamanda Ngozi Adichie: *We Should All Be Feminists*

Thomas Berry: *The Dream of the Earth*

Yolandi Boshoff: *The Starseed Sacred Circle*

Richie Bostock: *Exhale – How to use breathwork to find calm, supercharge your health and perform at your best*

Brené Brown: *Daring Greatly – How the courage to be vulnerable transforms the way we live, love, parent and lead*

Judith Butler: *Gender Trouble – Feminism and the subversion of identity*

Mariana Caplan: *Eyes Wide Open – Cultivating discernment on the spiritual path*

Rachel Cargle: *The Great Unlearn* (patreon.com/thegreatunlearn)

Glennon Doyle: *Untamed – Stop pleasing, start living*

Barbara Ehrenreich & Deirdre English: *Witches, Midwives and Nurses – A history of women healers*

L Harris (leahharris.medium.com/)

Yuval Noah Harari: *Sapiens – A Brief History of Humankind*

David R. Hawkins: *The Map of Consciousness Explained*

Valarie Kaur: *See No Stranger – A memoir and manifesto of revolutionary love*

Bessel van der Kolk: *The Body Keeps the Score – Mind, brain and body in the transformation of trauma*

Danielle LaPorte: *Core Desired Feelings*

Lisa Lister: *Code Red – Know your flow, unlock your superpowers and create a bloody amazing life. Period.*

Dr Shay-Akil McClean PhD: *The Hood Biologist* (patreon.com/Hood_Biologist)

Miguel M. Morales, Bruce Owens Grimm and Tiff Joshua Ferenti (Eds): *Fat and Queer – An anthology of Queer and Trans bodies and lives*

The Nap Ministry (thenapministry.wordpress.com)

Sheryl Paul: *Sacred Sexuality* (course via www.conscioustransitions.com)

Bill Plotkin: *Soulcraft – Crossing into the mysteries of nature and the psyche*

Rachel Ricketts: *Do Better – Spiritual activism for fighting and healing from white supremacy*

Spiritual Activism 101 and 102 (course via www.rachelricketts.com)

Rachel Rodgers: *We Should All Be Millionaires – A woman's guide to earning more, building wealth and gaining economic power*

Sonya Renee Taylor: *The Body Is Not an Apology – The power of radical self-love*

Meggan Watterson: *Mary Magdalene Revealed – The first apostle, her feminist gospel & the Christianity we haven't tried yet*

    The Divine Feminine Oracle

Alice Wong (Ed): *Disability Visibility – First-person stories from the twenty first century*

ABOUT THE AUTHOR

Ceryn Rowntree is a Medium, Therapist and Guide who supports clients re-connect to their own wholeness and bring themselves, their lives and maybe even the world back to a place of alignment, flow and sacred balance.

Ceryn's own journey to divine feminism began after a decade in high-pressured corporate jobs and a series of draining relationships left her burned out and convinced she wasn't enough. A practicing witch who had connected with the worlds of spirit and soul from a young age, she decided to turn inwards and follow the urgings of a deeper and more connected approach to feminism that was calling to her soul.

Ceryn lives in Northumberland, England with her German Shepherd Kali and is never happier than when the two of them are walking in the woods.